CW00607215

TEN The Observer SPORT MONTHLY

EDITED BY
GORDON THOMSON

YELLOW JERSEY PRESS
LONDON

THE GOOD

THE BAD

THE UGLY

CREDITS

Contributors
Denis Campbell, Euan Ferguson, Jon Henderson, David Hills, Lee Honeyball, Oliver Irish, Jamie Jackson, Duncan Mackay, Vic Marks, Pete May, Kevin Mitchell, Gavin Newsham, Oliver Owen, Simon Rae, Graham Rock, Matt Tench, Gordon Thomson, Graeme Thomson and Paul Wilson

Design
Pablo Juncadella, Friederike Huber

Text editing
Beth Coates

Photographs
All photographs © Getty Images, except: p. 37, Norway v England © Offside Sports Photography; p. 55, Fred Trueman © Granada Media; p. 56, Superstars © The Times/NI Syndication; p. 57, World of Sport © ITV Sport Archive; p. 71, Maradona © Offside Sports Photography; p. 124, Ronaldo © Paulo Whitaker/Reuters/Popperfoto.com; p. 140, Frank Worthington © The Sun/NI Syndication; p. 160, Karsten Jancker © AP; p. 173, George Berry © Offside Sports Photography
Thanks to Richard Pitts and the team at Getty Images for their help

I can't speak for you, but I wasted years on lists. Nick Hornby may have been the first to plead mea culpa to this peculiarly male obsession, but I too confess: I was a compulsive list-maker. Alone or with friends, at school or on buses, in my head and on the back of lined jotters, I compiled top 10 lists. Albums, B-sides, Scotland strikers, World Cup goals scored by Paolo Rossi and Zico, Grand Slam golf winners and, later, subtitled films and early-20th-century American novels (to impress the girls) were all thrust into a strict, often highly arbitrary pecking order which could change upwards of a dozen times during a single period of Maths alone. Lists set in stone in September would become completely unrecognisable by October. Seemingly indispensable midfielders and 'seminal' opening song lines would be ruthlessly purged, coolly crossed out and replaced with a new set of temporary favourites. There were some list deities that rarely dropped out of the top 5, let alone 10 (Dalglish, Maradona, side one of *The Unforgettable Fire*, Tunnock's Caramel Wafers) but not many: the kangaroo court in the playground saw that few escaped the drop for too long. It was fickle, but it was a lot of fun.

Today, lists are ubiquitous. A whole culture has sprung up based around them. There's virtually nothing which can't be reduced or simmered down into a tidy numerical hierarchy. C & W hits, minor *Fawlty Towers* characters, Joe Pesci's swearing, bottoms, breasts, bowlers, biscuits and FA Cup goals from Round 3. Ever since *Top of the Pops* made numbers 1 to 10 the digits to die for, we've become obsessed with getting rid of the rubbish cluttering up places 11 to 100 and making everyone fight for their place at the head table. Nostalgia TV shows have embraced the format but sport is the undisputed king of the top 10 feature. And the *Observer Sport Monthly* is largely responsible for putting it up there.

I've always loved the *Tens* in *Sport Monthly*. Before I began working on the magazine it was the first thing I turned to every month. They were funny, annoying, often wrong and nearly always brilliant. Now I am lucky enough to commission and edit them it's still the one piece I can't wait to read. I don't know anyone who doesn't love them, and I've yet to meet a journalist who won't duck a deadline to write one. Why? The brutally honest answer is, I'm sure, that they're the ultimate exercise in vanity journalism.

A *Ten* needs to be totally subjective, otherwise it won't work. The one rule a writer must follow is: 'Who cares what anyone else thinks, this is my list.' A harder task than it sounds, given that colleagues and friends are ever eager to hover instructively over one's shoulder once they've discovered you're working on a *Sport Monthly* list. 'Have you got so-and-so in there?' they ask helpfully. 'You can't have left *that* out...' Some journalists, the ones who clearly don't systematically stockpile Post-it notes, initially failed to grasp that this wasn't a test; there was no 'right' or 'wrong' answer lurking among the research notes. Nobody would laugh at their choices (OK, they might, but more frequently they would be laughing 'with' them) and, crucially, once they accepted a *Ten* commission it gave them complete freedom to dictate editorial policy for a page or two. Meddling editors would promise not to meddle (they would meddle, but not much).

There's always a price to pay for freedom, however, hence the bulging postbag of responses we receive every month (always more for the 'straight' lists, less for the 'funnies'). Loosely comprising persistent pedants, field experts and the obligatory anorak or two, the many readers who write in provide the magazine's best interactive service. I wish we had room to print more of their responses in this book. Instead we've cherry-picked the angriest, funniest, daftest and most passionate. 'Actually I Think You'll Find...' of Aberdour doesn't make it. D.C. Kneath, who has loyally mailed the office every month since Issue One, often more than once, does. Thanks, D.C. What would we have done without your frankly bewildering pleas for impartiality?

Ten has been imitated, plundered, ripped off, call it whatever you will; new lists of 10s continue to spring up in publications on an almost weekly basis. I know this because I've fumed at their exclusions, fought silent arguments with distant writers on trains and argued the toss with mute computer screens. I know who they missed. But then don't we all?

Is *Ten* self-indulgent? A random collection of superfluous facts and figures? Or is it a masterclass of contentious miscellany? I'm tempted to borrow the phrase a former editor of mine used to praise popular bite-sized journalism: *Ten* is a wonderful toilet companion; a great bog read. Whatever you think of *Ten*, I promise it won't fail to engage you. Hopefully it will also make you laugh, spit with rage and curse the man who first thought of stuffing information into random lists of 10. I blame Moses.

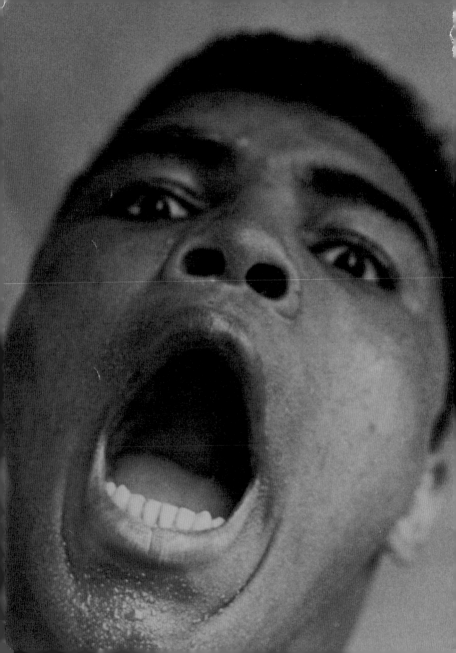

THE GOOD

THE TEN GREATEST BOXERS OF ALL TIME

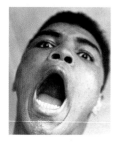

01 MUHAMMAD ALI
Heavyweight (1960–81)

'I don't think it's bragging to say I'm something special.' He wasn't bragging and he is special, still long after the end of his fighting career. What defines Ali as a man as much as a fighter is his courage. He took on the world and shook it when nobody gave him a hope in hell: against Liston; defying the draft; coming back at 32 to beat George Foreman; going toe to toe with Joe Frazier in that third, horrific collision in Manila; and then taming his Parkinson's syndrome. His serenity now comes from that almost unbendable fortitude. He lost five times, once at his peak, to Frazier, and later in decline. He probably got the benefit of the doubt against Ken Norton. But at his dancing, lightning peak, cutting down Cleveland Williams, bamboozling Zora Folley, there was nobody like him.

02 SUGAR RAY ROBINSON
Welterweight/Middleweight (1940–65)

Emanuel Steward picks him ahead of Ali, and there are arguments for that case. Chief among them is Robinson's length of service: 202 professional bouts between 1940 and 1965. He was welterweight champion between 1946 and 1951, and held the middleweight title five times in the fifties. Those who saw his early days, of which there is very little film evidence, say Robinson as a welterweight was untouchable. He hit equally hard with both hands and moved like Nijinsky. He also lived stylishly, enchanting all of Europe with an entourage that included a hairdresser and a midget, before Randolph Turpin caught him on an offday. Ninety days later, Sugar Ray got his revenge. In his prime, nobody beat him twice. Ask Jake La Motta.

03 **JOE LOUIS**
Heavyweight (1934–51)

It was Joe who inspired Sugar Ray Robinson to box, the younger man tagging along with him to a Detroit gym before his family moved to New York. The Motor City was some fight town, and nobody graced it better than Louis. His mother wanted him to be a violinist but the boxing bug kicked in and opponents fell like axed oaks. His 12-year reign as heavyweight champion was one of total dominance. Eddie Futch, who sparred with him, reckoned his jab and right cross were just about the deadliest combination in boxing. Joe's chin let him down a few times, but he rarely failed to get up and win.

04 JIMMY WILDE
Flyweight (1910-23)

The leek-thin Welshman was a freak of nature. He barely weighed seven stone and good fighters two stone heavier were reluctant to share a ring with him. Nobody's sure how many times he got through the ropes, as Wilde was brought up around the booths of South Wales, where he would often fight several times a day – and never lose. They called him the Ghost with a Hammer in his Hand, a clumsy *nom de guerre* that almost certainly would not fit on his little gown but one with which hundreds of victims would hardly argue. Boxing Illustrated once rated him the 10th hardest hitter in the entire history of boxing. He was flyweight champion for seven years when it really mattered, the best little man among several thousands.

05 BENNY LEONARD
Lightweight (1911-32)

For eight years up until the mid-twenties, he was the quintessential boxing master. His was the classic American-Jewish boxing background, raised on the tough lower-east side of New York City. By the age of 15 Leonard was boxing as a pro and he was phenomenally popular. The elegant but ruthless lightweight raised boxing to an art form and once said, 'The toughest fighter to fight is a stupid fighter. When you feint him, he doesn't even know you're doing it.'

06 ARCHIE MOORE
Light-heavyweight (1936-63)

The Ol' Mongoose had more moves than a bagful of snakes and showed them off against a huge variety of opponents over 27 years. Moore was one of those fighters so good nobody wanted to touch him. When he did get his title shot, he was light-heavyweight champion from 1952 to 1962.

Nobody knocked out more opponents: 141 in 229 fights. But he was not a vicious man, just very good at what he did. One of the true masters of boxing.

07 JACK JOHNSON
Heavyweight (1897-1938)

The big man from Galveston, Texas, endured all manner of insults and hounding by the white establishment to become the first black heavyweight champion. He was a remarkable man in many ways, a confidant of Rasputin, a lover of fine wine and poetry and the first boxer to leave behind the old centre-of-the-ring milling ways in favour of scientific boxing (forget James J. Corbett, whose reputation was inflated by the hypsters of the day). Johnson would have been terrific in any era, from bareknuckle to today.

08 SUGAR RAY LEONARD
Welter/Light-middle/Middle/ Super-middle/ Light-heavyweight (1977-91; one comeback fight in 1997)

The second Sugar Ray never doubted how good he was, with justification. A startlingly skilled amateur, he carried his pure boxing style into the professional ranks against the finest collection of fighters between 10 and 11 stone in the history of the game: Roberto Duran, Marvin Hagler and Thomas Hearns. Hagler fans (Manny Steward especially) will dispute it, but Leonard was the best of them. 'I want my fights to be seen as plays,' the former choirboy said once. He won world titles at five weights. What more can you say?

09 JACK DEMPSEY
Heavyweight (1914-27)

Few fighters had a better nickname than the Manassa Mauler. He fought like he lived: with total disregard for niceties. Dempsey might have been eaten alive by the big, sophisticated heavyweights of the modern era, but in his day he was a powerhouse nobody could hold at bay. Tyson cites Dempsey as his favourite fighter, 'an absolutely ferocious gentleman'. He would have beaten Rocky Marciano of the latter-day heavies around his size and might even have inconvenienced Joe Frazier, who was about his size. A trailblazer.

10 HENRY ARMSTRONG
Feather/Light/Welterweight (1931-45)

Hammering Hank, Homicide Hank – whatever you called him, Armstrong buzzed with energy that astounded onlookers and opponents. He remains the only fighter to hold world titles at three weights at the same time, a feat that boxing politics today would make impossible. From featherweight to welterweight, he must have thrown tens of thousands of punches in his 181 bouts, 101 of which finished early.

READER RESPONSES

Surely your list should have included Teofilo Stevenson – the only boxer the world dared to imagine might prove the consistent equal of Muhammad Ali, if they ever had been allowed to meet!
**J Mangan,
Ennis, Ireland**

01 Sugar Ray Robinson
02 Muhammad Ali
03 Henry Armstrong
04 Archie Moore
05 Jack Johnson
06 Benny Leonard
07 Sugar Ray Leonard
08 Julio Cesar Chavez
09 Jimmy Wilde
10 Evander Holyfield
**Tim Fredericks,
Crewe**

THE TEN MOST GLAMOROUS OTHER HALVES

01 JOE DIMAGGIO AND MARILYN MONROE

Still the ultimate pairing, despite the marriage lasting a mere 10 months. Both remain absolute icons of the twentieth (America's) century, even though Marilyn, who would have been 77 this year, spent her most famous years, after 1962, being dead, and DiMaggio stopped playing in 1951, three years before the wedding. Signs were inauspicious from the start. Marilyn broke off their honeymoon to go to entertain the troops in Korea, returning to tell him, with a naivety bordering on the tactlessly gauche: 'Joe, you've never heard cheering like it!' The baseball star was older, reclusive and, by many accounts, too close to the

Mob, and Marilyn's problems during these years have been exhaustively chronicled, yet the brief combination of a boy from nowhere with a golden swing and a girl from nowhere with an epoch-stopping wiggle, both making it big and winning each other, remains as close to fulfilling the American Dream as it gets.

02 LUIS MIGUEL GONZALEZ LUCAS AND AVA GARDNER (AND RITA HAYWORTH, LANA TURNER, LAUREN BACALL AND BRIGITTE BARDOT)

The impossibly flamboyant and handsome matador, who went in the ring by the name Dominguin, was the DiMaggio of Spain, but with added *cojones*. Apart from his three-year fling with Gardner – he once filled her room with 56 vases of roses, one for every year of the century – he had affairs with Rita Hayworth, Lana Turner, Lauren

Bacall and Brigitte Bardot, was fêted and immortalised by Ernest Hemingway, and on his farewell appearance in 1971 his suit of lights was designed by an artist chum called Pablo Picasso.

03 DAVID AND VICTORIA BECKHAM

The most 'of-our-times' couple of our times. They managed not simply to be glamorous and good – in one case magnificent – at what they do, but to rewrite the rules about footballers' relationships. After decades in which to be on the arm of a star striker was to define yourself by peroxide, white stilettos, tawdry 'glamour shots' and kiss-'n'-tell confessions, Posh 'n' Becks showed us, during those late-nineties days when women started to want men who could do soft hands and big jerseys, that it was possible to stay in love and have babies and live together and avoid all the interesting bits such as bitching and blackmail and suicide, and still somehow win the approbation of Julie Burchill. They pulled off a coup and the achievement should not be underrated. Despite the wedding thrones.

04 GEORGE BEST AND ... VARIOUS

Had Best been slightly less talented, charming and good-looking – you might as well say had the sea been a little less wet and salty – he might easily have fallen into the tawdry-blonde trap, especially given the number of times he had his beer goggles on. Well, he did, a bit: there was a fair slew of air hostesses and hairdressers and 'fashion models'. But Best's main blondes were, well, the best. Susan George...first wife Angie...former Miss World Mary Stavin...despite the feather-cuts and moonboots of the time, all were still of a subtly different class: they inspired not sneers but simple, bitter, heartfelt jealousy, in the way that his current wife, Alex, inspires gargantuan respect.

05 MARCEL CERDAN AND EDITH PIAF

The son of a Casablanca butcher who became the pride of France, the fast-punching middleweight (this is Cerdan, not Piaf) was described by Jake La Motta as the greatest boxer ever to come out of Europe. He confessed his adulterous love for Piaf before a mobbed dockside press conference in 1949, silencing the screaming reporters with his honesty and by asking them, at the end: 'Now I want all of you hundreds here to greet me, to harass me, to answer my one question: Have you ever cheated on your wife?' Four months later he died in a plane crash in the Azores. Piaf fainted on stage in New York the night she heard the news, just after starting to sing 'L'Hymne a l'Amour'.

06 BILLY WRIGHT AND JOY BEVERLEY

The Posh 'n' Becks of their day. The captain of Wolves – the Manchester United of their day – and England married, in 1958, the prettiest girl in the country's top-selling group of chanteuses. Self-effacing and immensely talented, Wright apparently tried to keep the wedding a secret, but 7,000 ever-so-politely screaming fans still turned up at Poole register office, in one of the first such displays of the celeb-worship we would come to know so very, very, tiresomely well over the next few decades. The last throw from a more innocent era and it's a fair bet that visiting fans didn't chant scatological ditties, possibly because it's hard to find many words to rhyme with Beverley.

07 JOHN MCENROE AND TATUM O'NEAL

Many like to view the new, mellow McEnroe as a sexier, funnier successor to Dan Maskell, after his winning commentaries, and he cringes himself when watching some of his early matches, but the eighties superbrat was still magnificent entertainment – not least during his tempestuous first marriage. They met in 1984 and married two years later, by when she had already won the nickname 'Tantrum'. Their public fights were almost as legendary as his playing, and they grew with his success; he wanted her to stay at home and bring up their three children, safe and secure with $100m in the bank; she wanted, not unfairly, to act. The end came in 1994; even McEnroe accepted he had been a 'jerk'. He took up the guitar and started sitting in on Greenwich Village sessions, which sounds sad and embarrassing until you realise he went on to bed Sheryl Crow and his current wife, Patty Smyth.

08 MARTINA NAVRATILOVA AND JUDY NELSON

The fact that all the other glamorous halves in this list are women, i.e. we couldn't find many high-profile sportswomen who drape themselves over beefcake, says much about the way in which successful men are attracted to looks whereas successful women appear attracted to such ridiculous conceits as love, humour, personality, etc. All of which were doubtless possessed by Judy Nelson, despite the fact that she had been a former Texan beauty queen. She was also a married mother-of-two when she met Navratilova in the early eighties and was instantly attracted. In the biggest shock to the Lone Star State since the Civil War, she left her husband of 17 years and toured the world as the tennis star's lover, travelling companion and $90,000-a-year 'maid'. They 'married' in Australia, but later split up and endured nasty and protracted settlement litigation, which soured, in hindsight, much of the consciousness-raising stuff they'd done for same-sex relationships when the world was only just becoming ready for it. Some of the world. Homosexuality did not become legal in Texas until June 2003.

09 ANDRE AGASSI AND BROOKE SHIELDS

American comedian Joe E. Lewis said of Joe DiMaggio, after the dream marriage to Marilyn went sour: 'It just goes to show no man can be an expert at our two national pastimes.' Sex and sport: can they ever mix? Agassi's career would seem to prove, dramatically, not. The high-profile Californian wedding, in April 1997, was dissolved within two years – a time that saw Agassi sink to 141 in the world rankings. Once it was over he started his exhilarating race back to the top spot. As the Americans say, do the math. Still, they were a lovely couple at the time; *Sports Illustrated* said they spent their wooing days 'like nuzzling deer'. Agassi, of course, is now married to Steffi Graf. Which only goes to show…

10 CHRISTIAN AND ADRIANA KAREMBEU

Despite George Best's world-beating action in the seventies our domination couldn't last for ever, and over the past few years the serious football–model action (as well as much of the best stuff on the pitch) has been the preserve of overseas players. Fabien Barthez and Linda Evangelista, Claudio Caniggia and Mariana Nannis, Zinedine Zidane and Spanish wife Veronique, even Sven-Göran and Nancy Dell'Olio (and Ulrika Jonsson). The laurels here, however, go to Christian Karembeu, formerly of Middlesbrough, now of Olympiakos, and wife Adriana Sklenarikova, the Wonderbra model. She even tried to take it on the chin after a mild press roasting for having dared point out that the food and weather on Teesside left something to be desired, but it was a bad time: the withdrawal of approbation from the Middlesbrough Eagle-Courant meant she was, sadly, left with nothing going for her except looks, brains, style, wit, sex appeal, money and success.

THE TEN GREATEST PERFOR- MANCES IN THE HISTORY OF ATHLETICS

01 ROGER BANNISTER The four-minute mile, 6 May 1954, Iffley Road athletics track, Oxford

For many years, physiologists said it was impossible for an athlete to run under four minutes for the mile, and the mythical time became so all-pervading that many athletes allowed it to inhibit them. By 1954, however, two men were determined to beat it: the Australian John Landy and Britain's Roger Bannister, a young Oxford medical student. Throughout 1954 they were running within seconds of the mark, but even so, when Bannister stepped out on to the small Oxford track in May the portents were hardly promising. It was cold and windy. Chris Basher and then Chris Chataway acted as pacemakers, with Bannister sprinting past Chataway 200 yards from the line, before collapsing. A calm came over the crowd as the announcer read Bannister's time: 'Three minutes…' The crowd erupted in cheers, drowning out what the announcer was saying. Bannister had run 3min 59.4sec.

Current world record 3min 43.13sec Hicham El Guerrouj (Mor)

02 **BOB BEAMON** Shattering the long jump world record, 27 October 1968, Olympic Games, Mexico City

After 1968, sports historians found a new word to describe a sporting feat that was dramatically superior to any that went before: 'Beamonesque'. In that year, at the Mexico Olympics, the American long jumper Bob Beamon jumped so far that the sighting device that should have measured it could not be used. Officials used steel tape instead, and it showed that Beamon had leapt an extraordinary 8.90m – fully 60cms beyond the existing record. Mexico City's thin air meant that a host of world records went at the Games, but by any standards Beamon's jump was exceptional. It stood until 1991.

Current world record 8.95m, Mike Powell (US)

03 **JESSE OWENS** Four world records in 45 minutes, 25 May 1935, Ann Arbor, Michigan, USA

Everyone knows about Jesse Owens's four gold medals in the 1936 Berlin Olympics, but his performance at a college meeting a year earlier was even better. He set three world records and tied a fourth, all in the span of 45 minutes. Owens had a bad back but persuaded his coach to allow him to run the 100 yards where he tied the world record of 9.4sec. Fifteen minutes later, he went to the long jump pit and put a handkerchief at 26ft 2½in, the distance of the world record. He then leapt 26ft 8¼in. Owens then set new world records in the 220 yards (20.3, beating the old record by 0.3sec) and the 220 yards low hurdles (22.6sec, beating the old record by 0.4sec).

04 **FLORENCE GRIFFITH JOYNER** Matching the men in the 100m, 16 July 1988, Indianapolis

A good, but not great sprinter, Florence Griffith Joyner in 1988 transformed herself into Flo-Jo, arguably the greatest female athlete in history. Her defining moment came at the US Olympic trials in Indianapolis when, wearing a dazzling one-legged running suit, she ran 10.49sec for the 100m. The time was two and a half yards faster than the existing record of 10.76sec, and better than the men's record in many countries. By the time she got to the Olympics in Seoul though, people were so sceptical about her performances that when she set a world record for the 200m, the press box remained totally silent. When she died in 1998 no one had come close to her time. They still haven't.

05 **BEN JOHNSON** The 9.79 100m,
24 September 1988, Olympic Games, Seoul

With his finger stuck up in the air and a disdainful look at his opponents, Ben Johnson had just destroyed the greatest sprint field in the history of athletics. The digital clock read '9.79'. Even now it's easy to recall the shock that reverberated around the Olympic Stadium in Seoul that day. The fact that it all turned out to be a trick pulled out of a chemist's bottle doesn't lessen that moment. 'Hey, man, I didn't do anything no one else was doing back then,' Johnson told the *Observer* in 2000. 'I deserve my place in history.'

Current world record 9.78sec, Tim Montgomery (US)

06 **EMIL ZATOPEK** Winning a third gold at the Helsinki Olympics, 27 July 1952

The Czechoslovakian army major had already won the 5,000 and 10,000m when he lined up for the marathon – an event in which he had never previously competed. He decided to run with the favourite, Jim Peters of Britain, on the basis that Peters should know what he was doing. But after a few miles Zatopek turned to Peters and asked, 'Are you sure we are going fast enough?' Attempting to psyche him out, Peters replied: 'No, we should be going faster.' At that point Zatopek took off to win his third gold medal of the games, the only man ever to achieve such a unique treble.

07 **FANNY BLANKERS-KOEN** Limited to four golds, 1948 Olympic Games, London

In 1948 Fanny Blankers-Koen was furious. A newspaper story said that at 30 she was too old to compete in the coming London Games. The Dutch mother of two duly competed in 11 races over seven days and was undefeated in every event. The 'Flying Dutch housewife' won individual golds in the 100m, 200m and the 80m hurdles, and anchored the 4x100m relay team to victory. The only reason she did not come away with more golds was a rule restricting individual entry to three events. She had waived the long jump and javelin, events in which she was the world record holder.

08 UWE HOHN The throw that changed the design of javelins, 21 July 1984, East Berlin

Few athletes can claim to have set a world record which has forced the authorities to change the entire nature of their event but that is what East Germany's Uwe Hohn did. He threw the javelin a staggering 104.80m, almost the full length of a stadium, putting the lives of spectators at risk. The sport's rulers responded by redesigning the javelin, moving the centre of mass forward by four centimetres which meant the javelin could not fly so far.

09 MICHAEL JOHNSON Smashing the 200m world record at the Atlanta Olympics, 1 August 1996

Michael Johnson is one of the most introspective, self-contained sportsmen in the history of athletics, but even he could not contain his emotions when he saw the time – 19.32 – for his run in the 200m at the Atlanta Olympics. His face is a mixture of joy, exhilaration and disbelief, emotions shared by everyone present that night. His feat even overshadowed his achievement in winning double gold at the 200m and 400m. A world record that will survive for 50 years.

10 WANG JUNXIA
10,000m, 8 September 1993, Beijing

Fuelled by a diet of turtle blood and a brutal regime of running a marathon a day at altitude by coach Ma Junren, in 1993 Wang Junxia set times that most top-class male runners would be happy to call personal bests. Her 10,000m time of 29min 31.78sec, set during China's national games, was front-page news around the world. A few days later Wang also set a world record for the 3,000m that still stands. No non-Chinese runner has ever approached her times.

01 **PHIL TUFNELL**
England (1990–April 2003)

There have been some poor and unproductive number 11s over the years but none looked so terrified as Phil Tufnell as he went out to bat against an international pace bowler. Clearly he'd rather have been at the dentist's. He employed all the modern equipment available – helmet, inside-thigh pads, chest pads – but still pain seemed inevitable. In fact, Tufnell had a reasonable eye for a ball. Throughout his highest innings – 67 not out against Worcestershire at Lord's – he kept smashing over extra cover. That was before Glenn McGrath played for Worcestershire; medium-pacer Stuart Lampitt was their fastest bowler. Tufnell's lack of ability with the bat cost him Test caps. But now the No. 1 rabbit has become the King of the Jungle.

Finest hour (and 21 minutes) 2 not out in 81 minutes in Bombay (the spinners were on). **Test record** 41 Tests, 146 runs, average 5.03.

02 **BHAGWAT CHANDRASEKHAR**
India (1964–79)

Chandrasekhar had more excuse than Tufnell to be terrified. The Indian leg-spinner played before the advent of helmets and his right arm was withered by polio at the age of five (he bowled right-handed, threw left-handed and – for what it's worth – batted right-handed, but not for long). In Jamaica in 1976, when the Indian second innings was brought to a close on 97–5 – a lead of 13 – Chandra would have been relieved; captain Bishen Bedi claimed that four of his players were injured so they did not have to face up to the fearsome quartet of West Indian pacemen.

Finest hour In 1978 the Australians presented him with a bat with a hole in the middle to commemorate his batting prowess. Chandra, apparently, was amused. Acquired a record four pairs in Test cricket. **Test record** 58 Tests, 167 runs, average 4.07.

03 **DEVON MALCOLM**
England (1989–97)

Was brave enough but appeared to have problems seeing the ball. He could hit it vast distances if he connected. Occasionally he did (see finest hour, below). More often than not he missed. Sometimes he frustrated opponents long enough for them to bowl short at him. Courtney Walsh, stretching the laws to breaking point and beyond, peppered him in Jamaica, and at the Oval in 1994 he was hit on the helmet by the South African paceman, Fanie DeVilliers. This prompted the famous Malcolm outburst, 'You guys are history', and 9–57 in South Africa's second innings. In those days a nasty conundrum for England captains was whether to bat Malcolm or Tufnell at number 10.

Finest hour Adelaide in 1995, when he hit Shane Warne for two mammoth sixes.**Test record** 40 Tests, 236 runs, average 6.05.

04 **POMMIE MBWANGA**
Zimbabwe (1996–2001)

The Zimbabwean swing bowler was, by anyone's estimations, abysmal with the bat. His figures are awful – though he did manage to up his average to 5 in his last season for his country – but mercifully his career was short. Perplexingly the Zimbabweans claimed that he knew how to hold a bat. There is little evidence to back this up. However, deep research reveals that Pommie averaged 31 for Dean Close School in 1995 (top score 72 not out). Test cricket proved a tad more demanding than the English public-school circuit.

Finest hour He made a stunning 8 against England in May 2000 at Lord's,his highest Test score, before he was clean bowled by Andy Caddick. **Test record** 15 Tests, 34 runs, average 2.00

05 **GLENN MCGRATH**
Australia (1993–)

No doubt the Aussies will protest that we have the gall to include any of their number, but McGrath (pronounced,

according to the ACB website, 'Magraa' just in case he sounds too friendly) is pretty useless. He tried hard to improve when Steve Waugh, the best possible tutor, took him under his wing. This summer, batting for Worcestershire, he did manage to record his maiden half-century in first-class cricket, but his Test record still warrants his inclusion here. He's brave though. Early on in his Test career, he adopted the policy of bouncing the West Indian fast bowlers in the certain knowledge that he himself would be liberally bounced back and that he was incapable of coping with the barrage.

Finest hour His highest Test score of 39 against the West Indies in Port of Spain in 1999, in which he shared a last-wicket stand of 66 with Jason Gillespie, out of Australia's total of 269. He was man-of-the-match, although his 10 wickets might have had something to do with that. **Test record** 62 Tests, 316 runs, average 5.96.

06 PETER SUCH
England (1993-9)

Another brave man, given his lack of ability. He tried like fury, steeled himself to get into line against the fast bowlers and occasionally astounded us. In one Ashes Test he took it upon himself to charge Merv Hughes, an odd thing for one of the most reliable and professional of pros to attempt. Like Tufnell he would have played more Tests if he could bat – just a bit.

Finest hour The longest duck in English Test history against New Zealand at Old Trafford in 1999. He lasted 72 minutes. **Test record** 11 Tests, 67 runs, average 6.09.

07 JIM GRIFFITHS
Northamptonshire (1974-86)

Our solitary non-Test player, but Griffiths's exploits with the bat for Northamptonshire live on in cricketing folklore. He was hopeless; in 138 first-class innings he averaged

3.33 and notched 51 noughts. But like most rabbits he enjoyed one moment of glory…

Finest hour It was the NatWest semi-final of 1981. Northamptonshire needed 13 runs off eight overs to beat Lancashire when last man Griffiths strode out to join Allan Lamb. One problem: Michael Holding was bowling. So there followed a duel that was realistically described as 'the best bowler in the world against the worst batsman'. Somehow Griffiths got something in the way during Holding's final overs and from the penultimate ball of the match, Northamptonshire won. Lamb scored the runs, but it was Griffiths who was carried shoulder-high from the field.

08 ALAN MULLALLY
England (1996–2001)

Has too much ability to be in this list. He can be the cleanest striker of a cricket ball. Supposedly laid-back and unflappable, he often loses his marbles with the bat in his hand – especially when playing for England. Wild swishes, totally out of order in the context of the game, result. The most damning statistic of all is that Devon Malcolm averages more for England.

Finest hour Riling McGrath in Melbourne in 1998 while scoring a vital 16. **Test record** 19 Tests, 127 runs, average 5.52.

09 JIM HIGGS
Australia (1978-81)

This Australian leg-spinner of the seventies and eighties, and more recently one of their Test selectors, was a poor batsman. However, he is inordinately proud of his record on the 1975 Ashes tour of England. During that summer he failed to make the Test team, but he played in eight first-class matches. Yet he did not score a run on the tour. He had two innings and faced only one delivery, which bowled him.

Finest hour He made his top Test score of 16 at Adelaide against England in 1979 before being run out. **Test record** 22 Tests, 116 runs, average 5.55.

10 **COURTNEY WALSH**

West Indies (1984-2001)

Just scrapes in. He's scored more Test ducks than anyone. He's hugely entertaining, a comic mime artist in pads in contrast to the clinically ruthless destroyer we see when he has the ball in his hands. He has been there when the West Indies have recorded epic victories, most notably alongside Brian Lara at Bridgetown when the Australians were beaten by one wicket in one of the greatest matches of this era. And occasionally he hits the ball massive distances. Usually he gets out, though he can point to the highest batting average on this list.

Finest hour An unbeaten 30 against Australia in Melbourne 1988. During this innings he outscored Desmond Haynes, Richie Richardson and Viv Richards. **Test Record** 132 Tests, 936 runs, average 7.54.

READER RESPONSES

Any list of rabbits should include Kevin Jarvis of Kent: 258 matches, 402 runs, average 3.58. Such a low average over a long career shows dedication to the skills of the true bunny. I remember a televised Sunday league game when Kent fans cheered every ball he survived. There were only four cheers. With regard to Jim Higgs, he once said of his batting, 'You can't turn horse shit into strawberries.'
Mark Finnigan

01 JUAN MANUEL FANGIO Argentina

Grand Prix career: 1950-8

World Champion: 1951, '54, '55, '56, '57

No other driver has won five world championships and no one has come near to his win-rate, close to a victory in every two Grands Prix. But, statistics apart, it is the manner in which he dominated the sport – and in such perilous times – that places him head and shoulders above the rest. He possessed sublime car control, steering on the throttle and wringing the most out of everything he drove. He was also the most intelligent of drivers, able to nurse an ailing car home. His racing philosophy was, memorably, to win 'at the slowest possible speed'.

Greatest race German Grand Prix, Nurburgring, 4 August 1957. A botched pit stop left him with a 50-second deficit, but he hurled his Maserati around the fearsome circuit to catch the Ferraris of Mike Hawthorn and Peter Collins with only a lap to go. In the process he broke the lap record on several occasions, recording a mark eight seconds faster than his qualifying time.

02 **JIM CLARK** Britain
Grand Prix career: 1960-8
World Champion 1963, '65

When he died at Hockenheim in 1968 Clark was only 32 and already a double world champion. He dominated the sixties, spending his entire career with Lotus. When his car was on song he often finished the first lap of a race so far ahead of his pursuers that observers thought there had been a pile-up on the far side of the circuit. Whatever he drove he made go faster than anybody else could.

Greatest race Italian Grand Prix, Monza, 10 September 1967. A punctureput Clark a lap behind the leaders but the Scot not only unlapped himself but did the impossible and snatched the lead from Jack Brabham with only a few circuits left - but on the last lap the fuel pumps on his Lotus failed and he was forced to coast across the line in third place.

03 **TAZIO NUVOLARI** Italy
Race career: 1924-48
23 major race victories

After starting on motorbikes in 1920, Nuvolari once won a race when he was suffering from two broken legs – he had to be tied to his machine. He moved to cars in 1924 and became a legend – 'the flying Mantuan' – driving a Bugatti before signing for Alfa Romeo where he was virtually unbeatable. Most famously, he beat the might of Mercedes and Auto Union at the 1935 German Grand Prix while driving an outdated Alfa. In his day there was no such thing as a world championship – had there been he would have won it. Many times.

Greatest race Mille Miligia, between Brescia and Rome, Italy, 16-17 April 1930. Nuvolari drove his Alfa Romeo through the night without any headlights so his rival and team-mate, Achille Varzi, could not see him coming. Three miles from the finish he pulled alongside the startled Varzi, grinned at him, flicked on the lights and powered to victory.

04 **AYRTON SENNA** Brazil
Grand Prix career: 1984-94
World Champion: 1988, '90, '91

Probably the fastest ever over a single lap, his record of 65 pole positions is unlikely to be beaten. He won three F1 titles (all with McLaren) – his single-minded approach and amazing self-belief made him a fearsome, as well as charismatic, competitor. His death at Imola in 1994 remains one of motor sport's darkest moments.

Greatest race European Grand Prix, Donnington Park, 11 April 1993. All Senna's genius came to the fore during the first lap. He qualified fourth, one and a half seconds off Alain Prost's pole position. But on race day it poured with rain and Senna was sublime in the wet. In the course of the first lap he picked off the three cars in front of him (Prost, Damon Hill and Michael Schumacher) and drove off into the distance. When the flag fell only Hill remained on the same lap.

05 **ALAIN PROST** France
Grand Prix career: 1980-93
World Champion: 1985, '86, '89, '93

'The Professor' won 51 Grands Prix (a record) and four world championships with a driving style that was so smooth it belied how fast he was going. His cerebral approach to racing meant that even if his car wasn't the quickest he was in a position to pick up the pieces if those ahead of him encountered problems – he always had an eye on the bigger picture.

Greatest race Australian Grand Prix, Adelaide, 26 October 1986. Needing to win to clinch the title, he qualified fourth in a McLaren that was no match for Nigel Mansell's Williams. But come the race, he preserved his tyres to perfection while others suffered on the abrasive surface. As the fuel load lightened he pressed on to win and clinch successive titles.

06 JACKIE STEWART Britain
Grand Prix career: 1965-73
World Champion: 1969, '71, '73

Formed a legendary partnership with Ken Tyrrell that brought three world championships. Hugely professional, very determined and incredibly fast, Stewart took over the mantle of F1's leading light after the death of Jim Clark.

Greatest race German Grand Prix, Nurburgring, 4 August 1968. In driving rain and on a lethal track Stewart left everyone in his wake. After two laps his lead was 34 seconds. By half-distance he was almost two minutes to the good. As others tiptoed around and stopped for clean visors Stewart kept his foot down and won by more than four minutes.

07 MICHAEL SCHUMACHER Germany
Grand Prix career: 1991-
World Champion: 1994, '95, 2000, '01, '02

The best of his era. When he retires he will merit a higher placing, but while there is no doubting his genius behind the wheel there are question marks. He cracks under pressure too often and his tactics can be questionable. But with five world titles to his name already, his place in the pantheon of racing greats is secure.

Greatest race Spanish Grand Prix, Barcelona, 2 June 1996. The weather was dreadful and he made a poor start from third on the grid, finishing the first lap in sixth place. But from then on he was breathtaking, charging his way through the field, hitting the front on lap 12 and then disappearing into a race of his own as others struggled to merely stay on the road. He won by 45 seconds.

08 **STIRLING MOSS** Britain
Grand Prix career: 1951-61

Four times a runner-up in the world championship, Moss never won the title. But any list of great drivers that excludes him is worthless. He got as close to Fangio as anybody and given some luck might have been a multiple champion. His career spanned the transition from front- to rear-engined cars and he was adept in both.

Greatest race Monaco Grand Prix, Monte Carlo, 14 May 1961. Moss, in a private Lotus, took the lead early and pulled away as the more powerful Ferraris got held up in traffic. They chased him down though, breaking the lap record in the process. Moss responded by matching their times and held on to win by three seconds after 100 laps of constant pressure.

09 **GILLES VILLENEUVE** Canada
Grand Prix career: 1977-82

Maybe the fastest driver of them all. His career was cut short tragically when he died at Zolder in 1982, and he was never allowed to drive a car remotely worthy of his talent, yet he still managed to get to the front and compete with men in far superior machinery. He believed that a racing driver should go as fast as he could and try to win races. He would have been a star in any era and was unfortunate to race at a time when cars didn't permit 'touch' at the wheel.

Greatest race Qualifying, US Grand Prix (East), Watkins Glen, 5 October 1979. Villeneuve's most staggering achievement. On a wet New York day many drivers considered conditions too dangerous to venture on to the circuit, but some did leave their garages in order to post a time. Villeneuve was in determined mood and decided to attack the track. When the times were published the Canadian topped the list by an astounding 11 seconds.

10 **MARIO ANDRETTI** United States
Grand Prix career: 1968-82
World Champion: 1978

The greatest all-rounder. In the mid-sixties he dominated sprint-car racing in America. He then moved to Indycars, winning the Indy 500 in 1969 and won his first Grand Prix in 1971 when debuting for Ferrari. He subsequently became world champion with Lotus in 1978. He then returned to the States and became Indycar champion again.

Greatest race Qualifying, Italian Grand Prix, Monza, 11 September 1982. Ferrari were in turmoil after Villeneuve's death and drafted in an ageing Andretti for their home race. Ferrari needed something to lift the team and Andretti gave it to them by producing one banzai lap, good enough for pole position. He finished third in the race.

READER RESPONSES

Why didn't you include Mike Hawthorn in your selection? A driver with style, panache, and the first Englishman to win a world championship – and that too in the Fangio/Moss era. Moss never won a title. The Ferrari that Hawthorn drove was too small for him, and he competed in a sort of mechanics' overall wearing string-backed gloves. Hawthorne was a hero of the fifties, which was a pretty depressing era, and unusually for the Brits a winning hero. He was blond, glamorous, and definitely should have been included.
Glenys Jenkins, via email

I was surprised you included none of the feuds between the drivers in this list. Gilles Villeneuve, who honourably obeyed team orders at Ferrari to allow team-mate Jody Scheckter to take the 1979 championship, was incensed when new team-mate Didier Pironi stole victory at San Marino in 1982 from under his nose as he was cruising to the finish line. Villeneuve pledged never to speak to Pironi again and remained in a state of mental turmoil until the day, a fortnight later, when he crashed and died in practice for the Belgian Grand Prix. Alain Prost became champion after running Ayrton Senna off the road in the last race of 1989. Senna reciprocated the following year by barging into Prost on the first corner of the last race to secure the championship. The antipathy between the two was so great that Prost retired in 1994 rather than face the prospect of Senna joining him at Williams.
Michael Marshall, Bromsgrove

01 **'Lord Nelson! Lord Beaverbrook! Sir Winston Churchill! Sir Anthony Eden! Clement Attlee! Henry Cooper! Lady Diana! Maggie Thatcher – can you hear me, Maggie Thatcher! Your boys took one hell of a beating! Your boys took one hell of a beating!'**

Said by Björn Lillelien on Norwegian radio when Norway beat England 2–1 in Oslo in a World Cup qualifier, September 1981

Lillelien's gloriously over-the-top response to Norway's unlikely victory over Ron Greenwood's side marked the high watermark of football commentary as social critique. Passionate, uninhibited and a bit weird, football fans everywhere from Scotland to Argentina knew exactly what he was saying: that there is no pleasure as sweet as beating England at their own game.

02 'Suddenly Ali looks very tired indeed, in fact Ali, at times now, looks as though he can barely lift his arms up ... Oh he's got him with a right hand! He's got him! Oh you can't believe it. And I don't think Foreman's going to get up. He's trying to beat the count. And he's out! OH MY GOD he's won the title back at 32! Muhammad Ali!'

Said by Harry Carpenter when Muhammad Ali beat George Foreman, October 1974

When Ali's rope-a-dope tactic exploded into life in the eighth round few people could believe their eyes, least of all it seemed Harry Carpenter. Just as he suspected Ali was teetering on the verge of defeat, a thunderous right hand did the unthinkable. Shouting to be heard above the din in Zaire, Carpenter's is one of the few pieces of sports commentary that does justice to the moment being described.

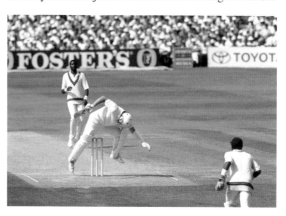

03 'He didn't quite manage to get his leg over ...'
Said by Jonathan Agnew,
England v West Indies, the Oval, 1991

After an attempted hook Ian Botham spun and became unbalanced as he tried to step over his wickets to avoid standing on them – but in narrowly failing to do so Beefy brushed the leg-stump with his inner thigh and was out. The gag, made by Agnew sitting alongside Brian Johnston in the radio booth, was the cause of much juvenile sniggering. 'Do stop it, Aggers!' Johnston was heard to splutter in the background while struggling to stifle his laughter. Reduced to tears the pair were barely able to talk for several minutes. Not everyone was amused though and they were, in true schoolboy fashion, banned from commentating together again.

04 'And Desert Orchid's beginning to get up as they race towards the line. There's a tremendous cheer from the crowd as Desert Orchid's gonna win it. DESERT ORCHID has won the Gold Cup. Yahoo is second. Charter Party is third. Simon Sherwood punches the air. Dessie's done it ...'

Said by Peter O'Sullevan,
Cheltenham Gold Cup, 1989

Not usually one to get too carried away, even O'Sullevan lost his cool amid the drama of Desert Orchid's Gold Cup win. Heavy ground and Cheltenham's stamina-sapping hill had never suited Dessie, yet as the grey improbably started to edge his way in front, O'Sullevan sensed victory and with the rest of the crowd stood to roar the people's favourite home.

05 'It is only twelve inches high ... It is solid gold ... And it undeniably means England are the champions of the world.'

Said by Kenneth Wolstenholme when England were crowned world champions, 1966

Not the 'they think it's all over…it is now' line you might expect from that match, but surely superior to the one that has become a tired cliché. Wolstenholme once told the *Observer*'s Will Buckley that he was much prouder of this line than the more famous one because it was replayed at Bobby Moore's memorial service in 1993. Which is good enough for us.

06 'The big Cuban opened his legs and showed his class.'
Said by David Coleman,
Montreal Olympics, 1976

The man who gave his name to a commentary cock-up (the Colemanball) could sometimes be so bad he was good. Like here, for instance. As Cuban Alberto Juantorena – nicknamed 'El Caballo' (the horse) for his muscular appearance and nine-foot stride – powered to 400m and 800m gold medals in Montreal, Coleman began his fine foot-in-mouth tradition with this observation.

07 **'And Damon Hill exits the chicane and wins the Japanese Grand Prix ... and I've got to stop, because I've got a lump in my throat.'**

Said by Murray Walker when Damon Hill became world champion, Japanese Grand Prix, 1996

Rather than select one from his vast array of Murrayisms ('The car in front is absolutely unique, except for the one behind which is identical'; 'Mansell can see him in his earphone', etc), this was the moment when Walker's favourite driver, Damon Hill, became world champion. 'It was the most emotional moment of my broadcasting life,' he said later. 'I felt everything welling up and thought, "Christ, I'm going to burst into tears." In my heart of hearts, I was worried that Damon wasn't going to get the job done.'

08 **'He's a poor lad.'**

Said by Eddie Waring after Don Fox's woeful miss in the rugby league Challenge Cup final, Wembley, 1968

The most dramatic miss in rugby league history, but where others might have banged on endlessly, this was all Waring said about Fox's woeful kick in the dying seconds. Somehow it fitted the moment, as if Waring did not want to intrude on Fox's obvious grief. As the Wakefield Trinity player sank to his knees, hands on head, he'd just handed Leeds the cup. Waring's reaction has now become almost as famous as the miss itself.

09 **'Oh I say.'**

Said by Dan Maskell at every Wimbledon for 43 years

Maskell was a commentator of few words whose golden rule was that 'a second's silence is worth a minute's talk'. In addition to the lovely 'Oh I say' he also favoured 'quite extraordinary' and 'a peach of a shot' as his other stock phrases. Not one for risking the unpronounceable, though, Maskell famously always referred to Martina Navratilova as simply 'Martina'.

10 'It's up for grabs now...'

Said by Brian Moore, just as Michael Thomas was about to score Arsenal's second and steal the title from Liverpool, Anfield, 1989

Moore at his brilliant best. 'In my commentating life I've churned out a few repeatable lines,' he later wrote, 'but this one, even a decade later, Arsenal fans are happy to use as a form of greeting. I was in a taxi driving round Piccadilly when the driver suddenly and joyfully started repeating the last full minute of my commentary that night. He knew it word for word.'

READER RESPONSES

It's the Parc des Princes, 3 February 1990, England beating France, Bill McLaren and Bill Beaumont in the commentary box. French television has always been bolder than us in its deployment of touchline microphones, so, as the forwards gather for a scrum, we hear loud and clear from the England hooker: 'No penalties, lads! Don't give 'em fuck all!' Which was glossed over, after an exquisite pause, by Beaumont: 'Brian Moore there, telling the lads to give absolutely nothing away.'
John Sheppard, Fulham

And, by courtesy of Norwegian broadcasting company NRK, the magnificent Lillelien rant in full:
'We're the best in the world! We're the best in the world! We have defeated England 2–1 in football! It's completely unbelievable! We have defeated England, England, the native land of giants! Lord Nelson! Lord Beaverbrook! Sir Winston Churchill! Sir Anthony Eden! Clement Attlee! Henry Cooper! Lady Diana! We have defeated them all! We have defeated them all! Maggie Thatcher, can you hear me? Maggie Thatcher! I have a message for you in the middle of your election campaign! I have a message for you: We have knocked England out of the World Cup! Maggie Thatcher! As they say in your language in the boxing bars around Madison Square Garden in New York: Your boys took one hell of a beating! Your boys took one hell of a beating! Maggie Thatcher! Norway has defeated England in football! We're the best in the world!' Beat that, Motty.

01 LASSE VIREN Fell in the Olympic 10,000m final only to get up and win gold in a world record time. Munich, 31 August 1972

At the start of the Munich Games, Lasse Viren, a 23-year-old Finnish policeman from the small village of Myrskyla, was not widely known. Indeed, the heats of the 10,000m were his Olympic debut. But when he stumbled and fell just before the halfway mark in the final his chance of victory seemed to have gone. The Tunisian Mohamed

Gammoudi (who had won the 5,000m at the 1968 Olympics) tripped over Viren and gave up two laps later. But the Finnish runner calmly got to his feet and chased his way back into contention, overtaking Britain's David Bedford, the long-time leader, to not only win the gold medal, but set a world record of 27min 38.4sec. Ten days later, he also won the 5,000m (in an Olympic record time) – a double that he repeated in Montreal in 1976.

02 HAMPSHIRE Bowled out for 15 and made to follow on, they went on to beat Yorkshire by 155 runs. County championship, Edgbaston, 14–17 June 1922

Headingley '81 is the best-known comeback in cricket history, but an even better one took place 59 years earlier. After Hampshire's collapse (they lasted 53 balls), they still trailed by 208 runs on the first innings. So confident was Warwickshire's captain, F.S.G. Calthorpe, that he suggested his team's amateurs play a golf match in the time left over once they had won the cricket. Lord Tennyson, the Hampshire captain, bridled at this and bet Calthorpe £10 his team would win – and won his money. In their second innings, Hampshire made 521 and then bowled Warwickshire out for 158.

03 CHARLTON 5–1 down with half an hour to go, having played most of the match with 10 men, they won 7–6. Second Division, The Valley, 21 December 1957

Huddersfield manager Bill Shankly watched in horror as Charlton's hero of the hour – dashing left wing Johnny Summers – engineered the most remarkable comeback in football history, scoring five and just for good measure setting up the other two. From being four down, Summers's goals – including a six-minute hat-trick – gave Charlton a

6–5 lead with two minutes left. Huddersfield promptly equalised, only for Summers to lay on the winner for John Ryan, who scored with the final kick of the game. 'Amazing, incredible, fantastic…' as one reporter put it at the time. Summers later revealed that he changed his boots at half-time after his old pair had started falling apart.

04 LARRY HOLMES Knocked unconscious by a punch, he got up to beat Earnie Shavers. World heavyweight title Nevada, 29 September 1979

When Holmes fought Shavers for the second time, he knew not to expect a quiet night. Shavers came to the bout with 55 knockouts in 66 fights and was regarded as the hardest puncher in the history of boxing. In round seven, Holmes went to throw an uppercut. 'That's when I saw a blinding flash,' he wrote in his autobiography. 'I was sure a photographer's flashbulb had gone off right in my eyes.' He had shipped a Shavers bomb. 'I was unconscious on the way down and came round when my head hit the canvas.' He staggered to his feet and, incredibly, won in the 11th.

05 HENRI COCHET Almost overwhelmed by Bill Tilden in three sets – then beats him in five. Wimbledon semi-final, 30 June 1927

F.R. Burrow, a famous Wimbledon referee, described this game as the most astounding event in his time at the championships. Cochet, a dapper little Frenchman, was being overpowered by the great American 'Big Bill' Tilden, who won the first two sets and led 5–1 in the third. Extraordinarily, though, Cochet, daring to take the ball earlier and earlier, won the match, 2–6 4–6 7–5 6–4 6–3. The spectators, said Burrow, were 'almost too spellbound to applaud'. Cochet, who had also come from two sets down to win his quarter-final, did so again in the final, saving six match points before claiming victory over compatriot Jean Borotra.

06 HERMIT A 1,000–15 shot, nursing a serious injury, he races from the back to the front to win the Derby. Epsom, 22 May 1867

Barely a week before the big race, Hermit pulled up with a broken blood vessel running in a trial at Newmarket. However, the rivalry between his owner, Henry Chaplin, and the Marquis of Hastings (who stood to lose £120,000 if Hermit won) ensured the colt's appearance in the classic. But with unseasonal snow flurries blowing across the Downs, Hermit's starting odds of 1,000–15 appeared a little miserly as he remained at the back of the field approaching Tattenham Corner. Suddenly he took off under the driving of jockey John Daley and at the winning post stretched out to beat the 10–1 chance Marksman by a neck. The Marquis of Hastings, it is said, went deathly pale.

07 DENNIS TAYLOR After losing the first seven frames of the World Snooker final he goes on to beat Steve Davis. The Crucible, Sheffield, 29 April 1985

When Steve Davis made his first significant mistake in the eighth frame, it seemed irrelevant. The world champion had won the opening seven frames, and Dennis Taylor was in danger of losing ignominiously. But Taylor won that eighth frame and so began snooker's greatest revival. He levelled the match at 17 all, and then won the deciding frame on a re-spotted black.

08 FRANCE Overcame a 14-point deficit in a World Cup semi-final to beat the mighty All Blacks. Twickenham, 30 October 1999

New Zealand led 24–10 after 44 minutes, so in statistical terms not Rugby Union's greatest comeback, but what elevated this remarkable victory was the awesome reputation of the vanquished. A 14-point lead seemed more than enough for the All Blacks, but in a burst of exhilarating adventure and cool kicking by fly-half Christophe Lamaison, France retaliated with 26 points in 13 minutes to win 43–31. 'This,' said Bill McLaren, 'was the greatest game of rugby I have been privileged enough to see.'

09 GARY PLAYER Down by seven holes in the world matchplay, he still wins. Wentworth, 15 October 1965

After 19 holes of his semi-final against America's Tony Lema, Player trailed by seven. From then on he was brilliant, but still two down with three to play. He retrieved one of these and then at the last hole hit a fantastic second, a wood that finished 15ft from the flag. He won a memorable match at the 37th.

10 BUFFALO BILLS Losing by 32 points, they still find a way to win. NFL wild-card game, Rich Stadium, 3 January 1999

The greatest comeback in NFL history was all the more remarkable because it was masterminded by Buffalo's back-up quarterback Frank Reich, not Jim Kelly, their regular play-caller and a notable escape artist. Trailing 35–3, Reich threw four touchdown passes, the last three to Andre Reed, to propel Buffalo into a 35–35 tie. The game went into overtime, when Steve Christie's 32-yard field goal sealed a stupendous victory for the Bills.

READER RESPONSES

In the second Test against Australia, in Calcutta, in March 2001, India needed 275 to avoid an innings defeat against the team on a record run of 16 victories. At 232-4, with Tendulkar out, the chance of a match win by 171 runs and a series win 2-1 looked remote!
**Richard Eccles,
Hythe, Kent**

You missed the 1999 Division Two play-off final. Man City, 2-0 down to Gillingham with 90 minutes up, drew level with goals from Dickov and Horlock in four minutes of injury time, and won on penalties. City thereby upstaged their bitter rivals who had come back from only 0-1 to beat Bayern Munich in some minor European trophy the previous week.
**Phil Neale,
Brighton and Hove
(Blue in exile)**

01 ARTHUR ASHE (US)
BEATS JIMMY CONNORS (US)
6-1 6-1 5-7 6-4
Wimbledon 1975

As the players came out on court, I remember being tempted to call out, 'Go easy on him, Jimmy.' Connors was the spit-in-your-eye kid who strutted the Centre Court with chest puffed out, at ease with the notion that he was invincible. With the bookmakers, he was almost unbackable at 6–1 on to win the final. But Ashe, an impressive man in every way, pulled off a breathtaking tactical coup, patting the ball at Connors who became increasingly frustrated as he tried in vain to generate a pace of his own. When a spectator exhorted him to raise his game, Connors's reply was full of frustration: 'I'm trying, for Christ's sake.' Later, Ashe delivered one of the great oversimplifications: 'He feeds on speed so I gave him junk.'

02 BJORN BORG (SWEDEN) BEATS JOHN MCENROE (US)
1-6 7-5 6-3 6-7 8-6
Wimbledon 1980

This would have been a towering contest, securing Borg's fifth successive Wimbledon title, even without the game's most famous tie-breaker, the 34-pointer that sent the match into a fifth set. Jimmy Van Alen, the American responsible for the tie-breaker, which Wimbledon introduced in 1971, had originally wanted it to be the best of nine points. If this had been adopted, Borg would have won in four sets when he took a 5–4 lead, but the tie-breaker provided a further 25 points of extraordinarily dramatic tennis. 'Lennart [Bergelin, Borg's coach] was white in the face, almost like a dead man,' said Borg's girlfriend, Marianna Simionescu, who was in the VIP box on Centre Court.

03 STEFFI GRAF (GERMANY) BEATS MARTINA HINGIS (SWITZERLAND)
4-6 7-5 6-2
French Open 1999

Until midway through this final, the quality of the tennis touched the heights. The second half was a Greek tragedy as the 18-year-old Hingis, who had led 6–4 2–0, went into emotional meltdown. Hingis, clearly affected by the fact that the crowd were so obviously favouring the veteran Graf, went to pieces after she was docked a point for unsportsmanlike behaviour when she marched round the net to dispute a line call. At the end, Hingis left the court before the awards ceremony, but was brought back, sobbing uncontrollably, by her mother.

04 **SUZANNE LENGLEN (FRANCE) BEATS DOROTHEA LAMBERT CHAMBERS (BRITAIN)**
10-8 4-6 9-7
Wimbledon 1919

Some women spectators were said to have walked out during Lenglen's matches because she dared to wear a dress ending just below the knee and with sleeves above the elbow. What is beyond doubt is that this was a wonderful contest, the 20-year-old Frenchwoman, who had never played on grass before, beating the title-holder and one of the surface's great exponents. Chambers was desperately unlucky when she held two match points in the 12th game of the third set and, as she wrote later, apparently had 'Suzanne in my bag of victories!' But she lost both to net cords and Lenglen, who was half Chambers's age, dropped only one more game.

05 **MICHAEL CHANG (US) BEATS IVAN LENDL (CZECHOSLOVAKIA)**
4-6 4-6 6-3 6-3 6-3
French Open 1989

So far, all the matches here have been finals. But this extraordinary contest was a fourth-round match between the mighty Lendl, 29, who had won the title three times in the previous five years, and Chang, only 17 years and three months and weighing less than 10 stone. After losing the first two sets and battling back to two sets-all, Chang was totally exhausted and it took two audacious ploys to win him the match. Serving at 4–3 and 15–30 in the final set, he startled Lendl with an underarm service that left the Czech exposed at the net. This so unsettled Lendl that he lost the game and went 15–40 down (two match points) in the next. Lendl's first serve was out and Chang tottered forward to receive the second midway between the service line and baseline. Lendl paused, missed with his service again and Chang was on his way to becoming the youngest male winner of a Grand Slam tournament.

06 CHRIS EVERT (US) BEATS MARTINA NAVRATILOVA (US)
6-3 6-7 7-5
French Open 1985

By 1985, Evert – or Mrs Lloyd as she was then – was into her 31st year and finding it increasingly difficult to withstand the awesomely powerful and athletic Navratilova. In the previous year's final, Navratilova had thrashed her 6–3 6–1 even though clay was a surface Evert particularly liked. This time, Evert re-established the primacy of her groundstrokes, but not before she had survived a memorable third set during which Navratilova rallied from 1–3 to 3–3 and from 3–5 to 5–5. 'Evert took her revenge [for 1984],' said one report, 'in a monumental match on Centre Court that honoured women's tennis.'

07 SUZANNE LENGLEN (FRANCE) BEATS HELEN WILLS (US)
6-3 8-6
Cannes 1926

Lenglen beat Wills, 'in a simple game of tennis, yet a game which made continents stand still and was the most important sporting event of modern times exclusively in the hands of the fair sex'. So wrote Ferdinand Tuohy in The *Fireside Book of Tennis*. Certainly the match made headlines around the world as the legendary Lenglen, 26, had to battle harder than expected to subdue the 20-year-old Wills, who would eventually succeed the Frenchwoman as the ruler of Wimbledon. At the end, 'the dukes and movie men invaded the court…and the limp and gasping Suzanne was held up in the midst of masses of floral offerings' (Tuohy again).

08 PETE SAMPRAS (US)
BEATS JIM COURIER (US)
6-7 6-7 6-3 6-4 6-3
Australian Open 1995

This quarter-final match started on Tuesday evening and ended, four hours later, at 1am on Wednesday. Sampras was emotionally and physically drained after his coach, Tim Gullikson, collapsed in the locker room the previous Friday (he would die from brain cancer the following year) and the exertions of a five-setter in the fourth round against the Swede Magnus Larsson. When a spectator shouted, 'Do it for your coach!' in the first game of the fifth set, Sampras started weeping. From then on, the match was a trial both for the player and the crowd as the title-holder fought against his tiredness and grief. Perhaps, though, the emotion sustained him, his tears seeming to provide the strength to survive an unforgettable struggle. He eventually lost in the final to Andre Agassi.

09 KEN ROSEWALL (AUSTRALIA)
BEATS ROD LAVER (AUSTRALIA)
4-6 6-0 6-3 6-7 7-6
WCT final Dallas 1972

Rosewall, the little master with the exquisite touch, had beaten his powerful compatriot in the first World Championship of Tennis final in 1971, Neil Armstrong, the first man on the moon, presenting him with the trophy after an exciting four-set victory. But his win the following year, when he was 37, was reckoned to be even better, the grace and economy of his play once again dismantling Laver's more robust game, although he took three hours 34 minutes to do so. The impact of his victory was heightened by the fact that commercial television in the US had covered tennis on a regular basis for the first time in the build-up to the final, which itself was watched by millions of viewers across America.

10 RENE LACOSTE (FRANCE) BEATS BILL TILDEN (US)

11–9 6–3 11–9

US championships 1927

Lacoste's demonstration of how great defence can win matches, even against an outstanding attacking player, which Big Bill Tilden undoubtedly was, left the 14,000 crowd at Forest Hills dumbfounded. The studious Frenchman, who kept notebooks in which he recorded the strengths and weaknesses of all his rivals, withstood Tilden's bombardment for nearly two hours, firmly fixed in his conviction that he could win the title for a second year. Tilden led 7–6 and 40–0 on his service in the first set, was up 3–1 in the second and led again in the third, 5–2, but Lacoste's superlatively controlled groundstrokes denied him even a set.

THE TEN DAFTEST SPORTS SHOWS

01 FRED TRUEMAN'S INDOOR LEAGUE
Yorkshire TV, 1973-8

A seminal pub sports show, *Indoor League* was one of only a handful of shows in the history of the small screen that made the nation's inveterate boozers feel like world-class sportsmen. The weekly showcase of darts and arm wrestling, shove ha'penny and skittles – car park fighting never made the cut – was overseen by England and Yorkshire cricket legend Fred Trueman, who, with pipe in hand and conspicuous absence of alacrity, talked us through the (in)action before signing off with a no-nonsense wink and his now legendary farewell, 'I'll si' thee…'

02 MIKE REID'S UNDER PAR
Discovery Home and Leisure, 2003

There were several golf shows vying for a place in the Ten. Obviously, *A Round With Alliss* came close but was excluded on the grounds that the last thing Peter Alliss needed was even more air time to wish the Major at Royal Porthcawl a speedy recovery. And Tim Brooke-Taylor popped up on cable recently in *Tim Brooke-Taylor's Golf Clubs*, wherein the former Goodie visits various golf clubs. It's as good as it sounds. Which leaves *Mike Reid's Under Par*. It features Reid defacing the nation's golf courses with a swing not unlike that of an axeman decapitating a king. Hilarious for all the wrong reasons, one need only watch the gruff comic carve another ball into the trees to make you realise that your golf game is not nearly as bad as you'd imagined. 'Triffic it most certainly isn't.

03 SUPERSTARS BBC, 1974-85

The autumn of 2003 sees the return, at last, of *Superstars* – the show for sports folk with nothing better to do with their time. It's long overdue. In its heyday in the 1970s, *Superstars* was required viewing. Whether it was Kevin Keegan falling off his bike, a drunken Stan Bowles shooting himself in the foot or Jody Scheckter's controversial sliding squat thrust technique, it was television sport at its very best; serious and stupid in equal measure and, above all, extremely funny. Can it ever be as good again? Well, with Johnny Vaughan taking over from the mighty David Vine, and a remarkable lack of seventies perms, it's always going to be a long shot.

04 SALMON RUN WITH JACK CHARLTON BBC, 1994

Long before Bruno Brookes hung up his Radio One headphones and cornered the market, grumpy ex-England stopper Jack Charlton tried his hand at taking angling to the British viewing public. The result was *Salmon Run*, a sad, sorry shambles of a show that was greeted with widespread critical indifference. Indeed, Charlton's unease in front of the cameras was such that observers noted that he need only pull on his waterproofs and waders and scowl at the River Tweed and the petrified salmon would voluntarily attach themselves to the World Cup-winner's hook.

05 **JUNIOR KICK START** BBC, 1982–92

Fronted by ex-Blue Peter stalwart Peter Purves, *Junior Kick Start* was a show you only ever watched in case some poor kid on an overly large trials bike came a cropper. Thankfully, that happened on a regular basis. Readers may recall the most calamitous clip from the show wherein one boy racer fell on the 'pole-over-the-hole' section and damaged not only his pride but his nether regions too, followed soon after by the St John Ambulance team who rushed to the nipper's aid and then lost their footing in the quagmire of a course. The programme eventually ended in the early nineties when a new generation of kids turned their backs on driving motorbikes over VW Beetles in favour of alcopops and joyriding. Purves, meanwhile, was last seen fronting Men & Motors' *Teen Trials*.

06 **WORLD OF SPORT** ITV, 1965–85

If the BBC's *Grandstand* was the first-born son that had flown the nest and found fame and fortune, *World of Sport*

57

was the cheapskate kid brother that was still living at home and sponging off his parents at 35. Fronted by the Terry Thomas of sportscasting, the rakish Dickie Davies, and set against a backdrop of really busy people bashing away on typewriters, it ran from 1965 to 1985, and was not only responsible for introducing commentating legends like Kent Walton and Reg Gutteridge but also presenting a wide variety of blue-collar events from old school wrestling to the World Bus-Jump Classic, where men in double-decker buses tried to leap over 100 motorbikes. Genius.

07 WORLD'S STRONGEST WOMAN
BBC, 2002

After two decades of covering hordes of hulking Scandinavian men with no discernible necks dragging juggernauts along a street, the BBC finally turned their attentions to the World's Strongest Woman in May 2002, when they presented the inaugural competition on the banks of the Zambezi, near Victoria Falls. From the moment presenter John Inverdale began with a desperate link between Dr David Livingstone and the contestants ('Livingstone,' he said, 'was more concerned with the abolition of slavery than with female emancipation') the tone was set for the most hilarious TV event since Margaret Thatcher left Downing Street for the final time. After the eight contestants had battled it out for what Inverdale called 'the coveted Butlin's Trophy', the critics rounded on the show, many to question the gender of the participants.

08 WE ARE THE CHAMPIONS BBC, 1978-85

We Are The Champions had everything: the comedy of *It's A Knockout*, the competitive edge of a school sports day and, in Ron Pickering, a giant in the world of sports commentary. Put simply, it was three teams of kids playing games with the kind of convoluted rules that made *3–2–1* look like a doddle. Each week, the games began on the playing field before heading indoors to the swimming pool, where, invariably, one kid could barely keep his head above water. Of course, the best bit came after the competition had ended, when in chaotic scenes not dissimilar from those at the end of *Titanic*, Pickering ushered the teams into the pool with his legendary command, 'Away You Go!', a catchphrase that was doubtless heard at his funeral in 1991 too.

09 **SKI SUNDAY** BBC, 1978–

Given that Britain has about as much of a track record in downhill skiing as Robbie Williams has in modesty, it's baffling why *Ski Sunday* struck such a chord with the public in its heyday. But what made it so funny? David Vine's colossal *CHiPs*-style sunglasses? The way enthusiastic locals in garish cagoules clanged saucepans as another downhiller hurtled past them and into the fence? Or perhaps it was the fact that plucky Brit skier Konrad Bartelski could always be relied on to come home a full calendar month behind Franz Klammer. Whatever the reason, *Ski Sunday* was strangely compelling – the often amusing events on the Hahnenkahm remain etched in the nation's memory.

10 **KABADDI** Channel 4, 1991–2

After the success of its gridiron coverage, Channel 4 turned its attentions to the subcontinent and the ancient Indian discipline kabaddi. To the uninitiated, kabaddi looked like nothing more than a bunch of barefooted Indian blokes playing tig in the sunshine. But then it did to the initiated as well. Sadly, despite fixtures such as West Bengal Police versus the Punjab, *Kabaddi* failed to capture the imagination of British viewers and as a result plans for further programmes based around playground games such as British bulldog and bikeshed smoking were soon shelved.

THE TEN GREATEST RACE HORSES

01 **ARKLE** Trained in Ireland, Born 1957, Golden years 1964-6

A steeplechaser so far ahead of his peers that the Jockey Club and Irish Turf Club had to change the rules of weight in handicaps to take account of his extraordinary ability. A superb jumper, he never fell, and was significantly superior to his brilliant contemporary, Mill House, himself one of the best chasers of the century.

Arkle was the son of Archive, a 48 Guineas stallion. He was bought as an untried three-year-old by Mary, Duchess of Westminster, for 1,150 guineas and named after the mountain facing her house at Loch Stack in Sutherland in the Republic of Ireland.

From the moment he won his first hurdle race at 20–1, Arkle appeared destined for greatness, usually with Pat

Taffe riding him. Perhaps his greatest victory was the 1964 Cheltenham Gold Cup when he avenged defeat by Mill House in the previous year's Hennessy by winning by five lengths, a race that Julian Wilson described as 'the greatest steeplechase of the past 40 years'. Until that race Mill House was widely believed to be the best steeplechaser since Golden Miller – but he would never again beat the great Arkle.

Roll of honour Cheltenham Gold Cup, 1964, 1965 and 1966; Irish Grand National, 1964; Hennessy Gold Cup, 1964 and 1965; Whitbread Gold Cup, 1965; King George VI Chase, 1965.

02 RIBOT Trained in Italy, Born 1952, Golden years 1955–6

Unbeaten in 16 races, this Italian-trained colt was sent out to land a King George and two Arcs at a time when the transport of horses was relatively primitive. He was tungsten tough, and for two seasons ruled Europe. His second victory in the Arc, by six lengths from a strong field, was one of the best in the history of the race.

Roll of honour Prix de l'Arc de Triomphe, 1955 and 1956; King George VI & Queen Elizabeth Stakes, 1956; Gran Premio di Milano, 1956.

03 SECRETARIAT Trained in America, Born 1970, Golden year 1973

Known as 'Big Red', this imposing colt was a Triple Crown winner whose performance in the final leg, the Belmont Stakes, was the finest in American racing; he won by 31 lengths in record time. A race was created to match him against the best of the age, Riva Ridge and Cougar, both winners of $1m in prize money. Big Red slaughtered them.

Roll of honour Kentucky Derby, 1973; Preakness Stakes, 1973; Belmont Stakes, 1973; Man O'War Stakes, 1973; Canadian International Championship, 1973.

04 **SEA-BIRD II** Trained in France, Born 1962, Golden year 1965

One of the easiest winners of the Derby, his reputation rests on his victory in the Prix de l'Arc de Triomphe. The 1965 race attracted arguably the strongest collection of middle-distance thoroughbreds ever assembled in one field. The flashy chestnut sweated profusely in the parade ring and then wandered alarmingly in the closing stages, but won unforgettably by six lengths.

Roll of honour Derby, 1965; Prix de l'Arc de Triomphe, 1965; Grand Prix de Saint Cloud, 1965.

05 **MILL REEF** Trained in England, Born 1968, Golden years 1971-2

The diminutive champion was outpaced by Brigadier Gerard in the 2,000 Guineas over a mile, a distance that favoured the winner. Raced over longer distances Mill Reef was unbeaten, and particularly effective on soft ground. Often he wouldn't just win, but win by a relatively large margin, as when he took the King George by six lengths. Brigadier Gerard won more races, but none of his achievements matched Mill Reef at his peak.

Roll of honour Derby, 1971; King George VI & Queen Elizabeth Stakes, 1971; Prix de l'Arc de Triomphe, 1971; Eclipse Stakes, 1971; Prix Ganay, 1972; Coronation Cup, 1972.

06 **PHAR LAP** Trained in Australia,
Born 1927, Golden years 1929–32

The best horse to have been trained in Australia, he dominated their domestic racing for three seasons. In 1932 he was sent to America, and contested the prestigious Caliente Handicap in Mexico. Another win, another record, but soon afterwards he died from poisoning. His heart is preserved in the Australian National Museum.

Roll of honour AJC Derby, 1929; Victoria Derby, 1929; AJC Craven Plate, 1929, 1930 and 1931; Melbourne Cup, 1930; WS Cox Plate, 1930 and 1931; Aqua Caliente Handicap, 1932.

07 **BRIGADIER GERARD** Trained in England,
Born 1968, Golden years 1971–2

Unfashionably bred, the Brigadier won 17 of his 18 races, being beaten only by the Derby winner Roberto at York in 1972, a race in which both horses beat the track record. A resolute galloper, he won the best 2,000 Guineas of the century, but many of his subsequent successes were gained against relatively weak opposition.

Roll of honour Middle Park Stakes, 1970; 2,000 Guineas, 1971; Sussex Stakes, 1971; Champion Stakes, 1971; Eclipse Stakes, 1972; King George VI & Queen Elizabeth Stakes, 1972; Queen Elizabeth II Champion Stakes, 1972.

08 **KELSO** Trained in America,
Born 1957, Golden years 1960–4

A gelding who was voted Horse of the Year in America for five seasons, Kelso won almost $2m, a record that was not bettered until more than 10 years after his retirement. His reputation for speed and durability was gained on dirt, but he beat the best turf horses in the Washington DC International of 1964.

Roll of honour Jockey Club Gold Cup, 1960, 1961, 1962, 1963 and 1964; Woodward Stakes, 1961, 1962 and 1963; Aqueduct Stakes, 1963; Washington DC International, 1964; Aqueduct Stakes, 1964.

09 RED RUM Trained in England, Born 1965, Golden year 1974

Winner of the Grand National in 1973 and 1974, he finished second in the next two years before completing a third victory in 1977 at the age of 12. A sound jumper, suited by a severe test of stamina, he took the Scottish Grand National in 1974. Red Rum had dead-heated in his first race, a seller on the flat at Aintree in 1967, 10 years before his final triumph.

Roll of honour Grand National, 1973, 1974 and 1977; Scottish Grand National, 1974.

10 **PRETTY POLLY** Trained in England, Born 1901, Golden years 1904-6

The winner of the three Classics, Pretty Polly would have added the Derby if she had been entered. She had the physique of a colt, she was beaten only twice in 24 races, and is the filly of the twentieth century.

Roll of honour The Oaks, 1904; 1,000 Guineas, 1904; St Leger, 1904; Coronation Cup, 1905 and 1906; Champion Stakes, 1905.

READER RESPONSES

Arkle was an exceptional chaser and easily the racehorse of the century. Red Rum, the Aintree specialist, and Desert Orchid, the King George specialist, deserve mentions for their impact on the public. Shergar, too, must be credited.

01 Arkle
02 Secretariat
03 Shergar
04 Phar Lap
05 Red Rum
06 Sea-Bird II
07 Istabraq
08 Desert Orchid
09 Mill Reef
10 Pretty Polly
**Michael O'Neill,
London E7**

No one who remembers Sea Bird is in any doubt that this was a peerless racehorse. There has surely never been a more facile winning performance in the Derby, but it is for the Prix de l'Arc de Triomphe that he will be best remembered. The complete authority and irrepressible turn of foot with which Sea Bird left the second horse Reliance toiling in his wake to win by an official six lengths leaves me in no doubt that he should be at the top of any list of great racehorses.

01 Sea-Bird II
02 Arkle
03 Secretariat
04 Tudor Minstrel
05 Mill Reef
06 Nashwan
07 Peintre Célèbre
08 Nijinsky
09 Night Nurse
10 Montjeu
**Steve Miller,
London N13**

01 MICHAEL HOLDING
West Indies, 1975-87

He was known as Whispering Death – umpires said that they did not hear the sound of his approach until he had passed them. The name alone was enough to strike fear into the heart of any batsman. Holding is responsible for the most devastating single over in Test history, bowled at Geoff Boycott in 1981 at Barbados. The England opener was beaten by the first five balls and then had his off stump knocked almost out of the ground with the sixth. There was a beauty and grace to Holding's destructiveness which raised him above the rest of the bowlers on this list.

02 JEFF THOMSON
Australia, 1972-85

Even in the West Indies, a fertile breeding ground for aggressive pacemen, they had never seen a bowler who could dish out chin music like Jeff Thomson. The former javelin thrower could generate frightening pace. At his peak in 1974/5, when he and team-mate Dennis Lillee roasted England, Thommo was a mesmerising sight: floppy-haired, big-nosed, hurtling in, the lean body winding up into a savage slingshot. Until last year, when Pakistan's Shoaib Akhtar hit the magic 100mph mark, Thomson held the record for the fastest recorded delivery, at 99.8mph.

03 ANDY ROBERTS
West Indies, 1974-83

Roberts was hellishly fast and perhaps the most intimidating of the West Indies' 'fearsome foursome', which also contained Joel Garner, Colin Croft and Holding. He was clinical and cold-eyed, hammering away mercilessly at a batsman's weak spot. It was said that he had two bouncers – the first was quick, the second was plain vicious. Sunil Gavaskar, the great Indian opening batsman, said 'Andy Roberts is the finest fast bowler I have ever faced.'

04 HAROLD LARWOOD
England, 1926-33

'You are my main weapon, Harold,' Douglas Jardine told Larwood when they arrived in Australia for the Bodyline

Ashes series in 1932/3. Larwood was the perfect choice for Bodyline – he was very quick and incredibly accurate. He was able to pitch the ball just about anywhere he wanted and shook up the great Don Bradman more than any other bowler. Larwood only played in 21 Tests, and never again after that famous series, but his surname remains an eponym for hostile fast bowling.

05 MALCOLM MARSHALL
West Indies, 1978-91

Marshall was a gentleman off the pitch, but a terrorist on it. At 5ft 9in he was relatively short for a paceman but he could work up a frightening speed if the mood took him. His bouncer spat at batsmen like a striking cobra, often off a good length (ask Mike Gatting, who had his nose rearranged by a Marshall special in 1986), and his heat-seeking inswinger was one of the most lethal balls in cricket.

06 FRANK TYSON
England, 1954-9

'Typhoon' Tyson, who had a penchant for quoting Shakespeare to batsmen, was not tall for a quick bowler but his broad, powerful shoulders enabled him to bowl blisteringly fast. He is rated by former Australia captain Richie Benaud as the fastest bowler he has ever seen. Tyson played a crucial role in England's 3–1 triumph in the 1954/5 Ashes down under, when he worked up a lightning pace on the hard Australian wickets, after being roused by a blow on the back of his skull when facing Ray Lindwall in the second Test.

07 PATRICK PATTERSON
West Indies, 1985-93

When Patrick Patterson arrived on the scene in 1985, Viv Richards warned the England tourists: 'You guys better liven up, this boy is gonna haunt you.' And boy did he haunt England, particularly at Sabina Park in 1986, when he bowled one of the fastest, most dangerous spells in Test history. Graham Gooch has since admitted that he was in fear of his life when Patterson steamed up the slope in that Test: '[It was] the first and only time I said to myself, "This boy is really flying and this could get very nasty."'

08 SYLVESTER CLARKE
West Indies, 1978-82

There has never been a more menacing bowler than Clarke. He did not have the intelligence to dismantle batsmen in the way that Malcolm Marshall and Andy Roberts could, and he lacked the style of Michael Holding and Wes Hall.

But batsmen feared him more than any of these. He was an old-fashioned, skull-cracking bowler, one who threatened not only a batsman's wicket but his physical health. He was once warned by an umpire for overuse of the bouncer, to which he replied: 'Dis no ladies' game, man.'

09 FREDERICK SPOFFORTH
Australia, 1876-87

It is perhaps generous to call Spofforth genuinely fast, but he was the first bowler to earn the nickname 'Demon', given to him not by journalists but by the batsmen he bewildered. The great W.G. Grace once said that however well he might be set, he was never sure that the Demon would not bowl him next ball. The aggressive-natured Spofforth was the first hero of Australian cricket, and took 14 for 90 against England at the Oval in 1882.

10 ALLAN DONALD
South Africa, 1992-2002

Donald makes the list chiefly for his explosive, unforgettable spell in 1998 against England opener Mike Atherton. Nasser Hussain, who was at the non-striker's end for much of the time, said that 'Donald bowled at the speed of light', which is pretty impressive stuff, especially with an old ball on a sluggish Trent Bridge wicket. This was one memorable occasion when Donald, always a fiery customer who loved to eyeball batsmen, lived up to his 'White Lightning' nickname.

THE TEN GREATEST WORLD CUP MOMENTS

01 THE GREATEST GOAL OF THEM ALL

Maradona's second against England, Azteca Stadium, Mexico City, 22 June 1986

The argument about who is the greatest footballer ever remains a live one (Pelé? Maradona? Cruyff? Carlton Palmer?); the one about the greatest goal isn't. Just four minutes after revealing his dark side, Diego Maradona made amends with a goal that perfectly expressed football's link between the playground and the World Cup stadium. On he went, slaloming England defenders on a run that began in his own half and ended in a global celebration. 'Which planet are you from?' screamed the Argentine commentator Victor Hugo Morales, whose hyperbole was for once justified. 'I am going to cry! Oh, my God! How beautiful soccer is! What a goal! Diego Maradona! You make it seem so easy! I am crying, forgive

me please!' Once the dust had settled, the cynical sought to belittle the achievement by portraying England's defenders that day – Sansom, Fenwick and Butcher in particular – as statuesque morons. That was unfair. All three were terrific players but in any case it ignores a more fundamental truth: Maradona on that magical, mystical run would have beaten anybody.

02 HAIL THE BOY WONDER
Michael Owen's solo goal against Argentina, Stade Geoffroy Guichard, St Etienne, France, 30 June 1998

Did anyone ever think any Englishman could capture the imagination in the manner of Maradona, let alone an 18-year-old? Yet on a sultry night in south-east France, a fresh-faced youngster from Chester did something that evaded the likes of Bobby Charlton and Bobby Moore. He took the world's breath away. Owen ran past Argentine defenders with the same ease that Maradona had evaded their English counterparts 12 years earlier, and if anything his finish was even better. Even the opposition could only applaud. 'The match,' wrote the reporter from *La Nacion* in Buenos Aires, 'was defined by the genius of Owen.'

03 GERMANY 1 ENGLAND 5
Olympiastadion, Munich, 1 September 2001

Is it cheating a bit to include a moment from the qualifiers? Who cares. For nearly 30 years, matches between England and Germany (or West Germany as they were for most of that period) had carried with them one, terrible undermining subtext: the Germans would always win. The assumption held good throughout and beyond a sustained period of Germany superiority and well into the nineties when, twice, England played better, but the Germans were better at taking penalties. It even endured beyond England's victory over Germany in Euro 2000 (a mind-bogglingly terrible game, between two mind-bogglingly terrible teams) and normal service was resumed four months later when the Germans won at Wembley. But in Munich in September 2001 came the most glorious of redemptions. Not just an England victory, but a dazzling, stunning, overwhelming triumph for the ages. And don't think that it was just the English that were celebrating.

04 'SOME PEOPLE ARE ON THE PITCH'
Wembley Stadium, London, 30 July 1966
You have to be over 40 for this to be a true memory, but for those that are the moment is indelible. Thirteen years after the Hungarians had taught the English a fundamental (and overdue) lesson, the nation that had given football to the world proved itself the best (the Hungarians having gone out to the Soviet Union in the quarter-finals).

05 THE FINAL FLOURISH
Brazil's last goal against Italy, Azteca Stadium, Mexico City, 21 June 1970
It may only be number five, but this moment retains a golden haze all of its own. It's something to do with clips from 1970: a combination of colour television in its infancy and the burning hot sun of Mexico in high summer make them shimmer with TV's equivalent of the sepia tint. And then there is the moment itself – the final flourish from the greatest team to play the game.

06 ENGLAND PAY THE PENALTY
Pearce's and Waddle's misses, Stadio Delle Alpi, Turin, 4 July 1990
Suffering. There can be no joy in football without it, and sometimes the moments of torture are the most memorable. Like this one. After an epic encounter it all came

down to five stupid kicks from the penalty spot. And as we waited for the exquisite pain of it all, every Englishman hoped for the best but sensed the worst. Do you remember who scored the England penalties that night? (Lineker, Beardsley, Platt.) But you certainly do remember who missed them.

07 ONLY BERGKAMP CAN DO THIS
**Holland's winner against Argentina,
Stade Velodrome, Marseille, 4 July 1998**
Filbert Street, Leicester. It doesn't usually have much to do with the World Cup, but it was the laboratory at which this exquisite moment was created. For it was there in a league match in August 1997 that Dennis Bergkamp first conjured a goal that perfectly demonstrated his lethal combination of gravity-defying close control and supreme coolness inside the six-yard box. Ten months later he did it again, but this time in the final minute of a vital game at the World Cup finals. The goal for Arsenal had been good but as Bergkamp's team-mate Marc Overmars said: 'This was not Filbert Street on a Wednesday night. This was a goal that won a World Cup quarter-final.'

08 THE HAND OF GOD
Azteca Stadium, Mexico City, 22 June 1986
It was cheating, but it was cheating for a reason. That, at least, was Maradona's view, one he emphasised when talking to *Rolling Stone* magazine in 1999. 'We told ourselves before the game that football had nothing to do with the Falklands War, but we knew intimately that Argentinians had been killed there, that they killed [us] like little birds. We blamed the English players for everything that had happened. Of course I know that's stupid but that's how we felt and it was a feeling stronger than us all.'

09 SENDING THE WORLD THE WRONG WAY

Pelé's dummy against Uruguay, Estadio Jalisco, 17 June 1970

If the footballing gods got just about everything right in 1970, they got two things wrong: Pelé's shot from his own half against Czechoslovakia, and this irresistible dummy on Mazurkiewicz, the Uruguay goalkeeper. Neither went in, proving if nothing else that moments don't have to be perfect to be memorable.

10 IRISH EUPHORIA

The penalty shoot-out v Romania, Stadio Luigi Ferraris, Genoa, 25 June 1990

Throughout a long and distinguished career David O'Leary was good at many things: heading, tackling, reading the game, looking a lot younger than he was. But no one ever thought of him as a penalty taker, until he had to take the vital kick in the shoot-out against Romania. But after an age a nervous centre-half was transformed into a cool, confident match-winner. 'I cried,' Roddy Doyle wrote in the *Observer*. 'It wasn't the winning, it was the sight of the squad charging towards David O'Leary; it was David O'Leary standing waiting for them; it was Packie Bonner with his hand covering his eyes, almost afraid to smile; it was the physio Mick Byrne's tracksuit top flapping as he ran up to David O'Leary; it was the sight of the Irish crowd in Genoa; it was the crowd here in the pub. It was being Irish.'

GOALS, SONGS, HAIRCUTS: 90 MORE MEMORABLE MOMENTS FROM THE WORLD CUP

THE BAD

THE TEN WORST PENALTY MISSES

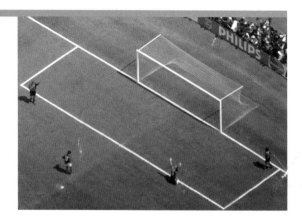

01 ROBERTO BAGGIO
Italy v Brazil, Los Angeles, 1994

The divine ponytail will now never win a World Cup, so it will probably be his misfortune to be remembered for losing one. The stakes could hardly have been higher as Baggio the Buddhist stepped up. Not only had Claudio Taffarel just made a crucial save to put the onus of an entire World Cup on the next kick, he had dedicated it to his Christian God by pointing to the sky. Baggio's shot went in that direction, bringing a disappointing World Cup final to an abrupt but appropriate conclusion.

02 JOINT AWARD TO STUART PEARCE, CHRIS WADDLE, GARETH SOUTHGATE, PAUL INCE AND DAVID BATTY

Gazza cries and Pavarotti warbled once again as England wake up to how good they really are under Bobby Robson and push the West Germans all the way in a semi-final in Turin in 1990 at the Stadio delle Alpi. An expectant nation remains optimistic when the game goes to penalties, not yet realising what the next 10 years will hold, but we begin to get the picture when Pearce strikes the fourth penalty against Bodo Illgner's legs and Waddle balloons the fifth over the bar.

Six years later it's England against the whole of Germany in the Euro 96 semi-finals at Wembley. People were expecting England to lose on penalties this time, realising that Germany were unlikely to be as generous from the spot as Spain had been in the quarter-final, which was partly why Southgate's body language seemed to say 'Why me?' from the start. The Aston Villa defender was hoping he would not be required, but it fell to this extremely occasional striker to take the first sudden-death penalty when the initial phase finished 5–5. Southgate missed, or rather Andreas Kopke saved, and Germany had arranged matters so that their experienced captain Andy Moller was available to score from the next kick and book another final at England's expense.

Two years later it's Argentina at France 98, and after a thrilling game which England were unlucky not to win in normal time, the expectation was that the penalty shoot-out would end in tears. So it did, with penalty tyro Batty attracting more criticism than Ince, who was the first England player to miss. The plain truth is that England did not have enough penalty experts on the pitch at the end, partly due to David Beckham's infamous dismissal. But Glenn Hoddle's contention that this was the best prepared England World Cup side ever looked a little glib when it emerged that his squad had never practised taking penalties.

03 DIDIER SIX AND MAXIME BOSSIS
France v West Germany, Seville, 1982

An earlier semi-final with the World Cup's first ever shoot-out and arguably its greatest miscarriage of justice. No real blame attaches to Six and Bossis for missing their kicks, the villain of the piece was Harald Schumacher, the

German goalkeeper who saved them. Schumacher should have been dismissed minutes from the end of normal time for a vicious professional foul which denied France a winning goal and put Patrick Battiston in hospital. Incredibly, he was not even penalised, and stayed on to see Germany through the shoot-out after coming back from 3–1 down in extra time. Small consolation for the glorious French side of Platini, Giresse and Tigana that Italy won the final, or that France won the European Championship two years later.

04 GEOFF HURST
West Ham v Stoke City, 1971

Having lost the home game of the two-legged League Cup semi-finals 2–1 in early December 1971, Stoke needed to win at Upton Park to go through to their first major final. John Ritchie put them ahead and in those days away goals counted for nothing so extra time was played. To the delight of the home fans – and disgust of Gordon Banks – the Hammers were awarded a penalty. The England legend then made a stupendous save from his World Cup-winning team-mate. Two replays later the Potteries side went through (despite a penalty save from Bobby Moore filling in for Bobby Ferguson in the West Ham goal) and Banks's save brought its full reward when Stoke beat Chelsea in the final to claim their first – and only – major trophy.

05 VICTOR IKPEBA
Nigeria v Cameroon 2000

The miss that wasn't – and it cost Nigeria the African Nations Cup. One of the worst refereeing decisions ever witnessed (and the linesman was most to blame as he was standing on the byline) handed the cup to Cameroon, much to the dismay of a packed crowd in Lagos. After a 2–2 draw the game went to a shoot-out. With the score 3–2 to

Cameroon, Ikpeba, who plays for Borussia Dortmund, struck his shot against the underside of the bar. It clearly crossed the line by about a foot, but the Tunisian referee, Mourad Daami, said, 'No goal.' The complaints on a BBC African website would take a tree to turn into print.

06 LIU YING
USA v China, Los Angeles, 1999

The women's World Cup may still be some way from attracting the same interest as the men's (though not in America), but at least its finals can be decided the same way. The defining motif of the 1999 Women's World Cup was Brandi Chastain in her sports bra, shirt waved in triumph above her head, after burying the USA's fifth, and winning penalty. The goat of the piece was China's Liu Ying, who had taken the third spot-kick for her country. The midfielder placed it to Briana Scurry's left but not far enough. The American keeper guessed right and palmed the ball away. For Team USA the only miss of the shootout made legends of them all. For Liu Ying from Beijing there were only tears.

07 JOHN ALDRIDGE
Liverpool v Wimbledon, Wembley, 1988

Of all the FA Cup finals in which to miss a penalty, it had to be this one. As soon as one or two high-minded observers of the game expressed the view that it would be bad for football were the Crazy Gang to beat Anfield's Quality Street collection in such a major showpiece, Wimbledon seemed fated to defy the odds and accomplish the unthinkable. Never more so than when Dave 'Lurch' Beasant saved Aldridge's penalty to preserve the lead Lawrie Sanchez had given the underdogs, who went on to win 1–0. 'No complaints,' said Liverpool manager Kenny Dalglish. 'I thought it was a soft penalty award anyway.'

08 DENNIS BERGKAMP
Arsenal v Manchester United, Villa Park, 1999

This was the penalty which could have put Arsenal into a second successive FA Cup final and stopped Manchester United's Treble in its tracks. Still slugging it out with United in the League, Arsenal had held them to a draw in the first FA Cup semi-final, and appeared to have the replay sewn up when their opponents first lost Roy Keane and then conceded a penalty in injury time. Peter Schmeichel was equal to Bergkamp's kick, however, allowing Ryan Giggs to supply the extra-time heroics and United to reach for glory.

09 BILLY AUSTIN
Manchester City v Newcastle United, 1926

On the last day of the 1925/6 season Manchester City went to Newcastle needing a point to avoid relegation from the First Division. A run of four consecutive wins suggested they would do so. They were awarded a penalty, only for outside-right Billy Austin to miss it. It proved a crucial error: Newcastle won 3–2 and City went down. It had been a bad week for them. A week earlier Bolton had beaten them in the FA Cup final.

10 ANY PENALTY TAKEN BY THE CORINTHIANS

The famous amateur side used to miss penalties on purpose, or tap the ball lightly back to the goalkeeper, believing that as all foul play was accidental it would be unsporting to take an unfair advantage from the penalty spot. Any resemblance between this archaic philosophy and Manchester City's penalty record is entirely coincidental, apparently.

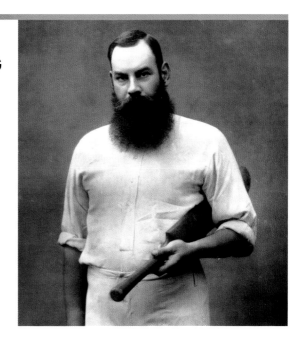

01 W.G. GRACE
England, played first-class cricket between 1864 and 1908

The godfather of gamesmanship. Tyrannical, domineering, intimidating, W.G. never missed a chance to swing a match his way. Peaks in a long career of sharp practice include kidnapping Billy Midwinter from Lord's in 1878 when he was padded up to open the Australian innings against Middlesex and taking him across the river to play for Gloucestershire at the Oval, and, four years later, luring Sammy Jones out of his ground and running him out during the Australians' second innings in the season's only Test. This backfired spectacularly as it so incensed the 'Demon', Fred Spofforth, that he took 7 for 44 to win the match for Australia. The shock was such that it gave rise to the spoof obituary for English cricket and the creation of the Ashes.

02 DOUGLAS JARDINE
England, 1920-33

Though from a different social drawer from Grace (Winchester and Oxford), Jardine played just as hard. Determined to cut Don Bradman down to size, he developed Bodyline, and had the iron will to persist with it, regally ignoring the baying of the outraged Australian crowds and the storm of telegrams and anger that it engendered at official level. When Harold Larwood felled the Australian captain Woodfull in the third Test at Adelaide, Jardine called out loud and clear: 'Well bowled, Harold.' Mounted police were drafted in behind the pavilion to quell the expected riot.

03 DON BRADMAN
Australia, 1927-49

Not an obvious choice as the Don was always regarded as playing it hard but fair. Like all Australians he only walked when the car broke down, but his decision to stand his ground in the first Test at Brisbane in 1946/7 caused a furore. He had struggled to 28 when he edged a ball to Jack Ikin who took it shoulder-high at second slip. When he stayed put, the umpire reprieved him. 'A fine bloody way to start a series,' muttered the England captain, Wally Hammond. Bradman went on to score 187, to win the Test and the series.

04 A.C. MACLAREN
England, 1890-1923

Another lordly England captain, whose airs both on and off the pitch antagonised many. Having set the world record first-class score of 424 at Taunton in 1895 (against a Somerset team comprising nine amateurs, including one parson and two doctors), he strenuously challenged the first-class status of the match in which the Australian Bill Ponsford eclipsed him with 429 in 1922/3. When the new record appeared in *Wisden* he tried to pull rank on the editor, writing furiously that he was 'reporting it to MCC'.

05 V.H. MANKAD
India, 1935-62
The great Indian all-rounder blotted his copybook in the second Test at Sydney in 1947/8 when he ran out Billy Brown at the bowler's end without first cautioning him. In mitigation, he had warned the same batsman against backing up too enthusiastically in a previous match. Nevertheless, he remains the only cricketer to have a particular sporting malpractice named after him. To this day in Australia, a bowler's run-out is known as a 'Mankad'.

06 DENNIS LILLEE
Australia, 1969-88
A dedicated sledger on the pitch, the fearsome fast bowler took intimidation a step further when, during Mike Denness's ill-fated tour of 1974/5, he used a television interview to put the frighteners on 'that little weasel, [Keith] Fletcher. I know you are watching and I will sort you out tomorrow.' He did. Then there was the infamous aluminium bat and accompanying tantrum at Perth in 1979/80, followed soon after by the very public kick directed at Pakistan captain Javed Miandad. And, of course, that little flutter on England to win at Headingley in 1981.

07 SALEEM YOUSUF
Pakistan, 1978-97
The Pakistan wicketkeeper who in 1987 contributed to an acrimonious series against England by claiming a catch off

Ian Botham when it was clear he took it on the half-volley. Far from reprimanding him, the tour manager said pressurising the umpire was 'a technique for all cricket teams' that 'has now become absolutely necessary in professional cricket today'. Mike Gatting's confrontation with Shakoor Rana followed within a matter of months.

08 GREG CHAPPELL
Australia, 1966-84

In February 1981 at the MCG in Melbourne, Greg ordered his younger brother, Trevor, to bowl a grubber last ball of a one-day international to deny New Zealand – in the form of tailender Brian McKechnie – any chance of hitting the six they needed to tie the game. The New Zealand Prime Minister called it 'cowardly'. Even elder brother Ian Chappell asked, 'How low can you go?' A rare stain on a fine career.

09 BRIAN ROSE
England, 1969-87

Two years before Greg Chappell's infamous order, Englishman Brian Rose succumbed to a similar clouding of judgement when the Somerset side he was captaining were playing Worcestershire in the Benson and Hedges Cup at Worcester. The game was the last in a round-robin mini-league that preceded the knockout rounds of the cup and Rose had worked out that provided Somerset lost no wickets, their superior strike rate would ensure that they went through, whatever the result of the match. Losing it was irrelevant. So he declared Somerset's innings closed after just one over, leaving the embarrassed hosts to score just two to win. This act of high bounderism got its just deserts when Somerset were swiftly and ignominiously expelled from the competition.

10 WARWICK ARMSTRONG
Australia, 1898–1922

Australia's most successful captain of the pre-Bradman era, Armstrong pioneered negative leg-side bowling, and in his country's triumphant tour of 1921 used his fast-bowling duo MacDonald and Gregory with bone-jarring ruthlessness. At the Oval in 1909 he bowled practice balls for 18 minutes while Frank Woolley waited to face his first delivery in a Test match. Not for nothing was he known as 'the Australian W.G.'.

READER RESPONSES

The inclusion of Brian Rose is a travesty of justice. If Rose played for Surrey or Yorkshire he would be lauded as a tactical genius, but because he captained, very successfully, an unfashionable side he was pilloried. Where are all the ball tamperers and pitch doctorers that were conlemporary with Rose such as the Essex bowlers or Nottinghamshire groundstaff?
**Keith Sellick,
London**

I detect an overdose of political correctness and a shortage of accuracy in your choice. So Douglas Jardine invented and applied the Bodyline theory? He was not infringing any of the playing laws of the time, and indeed some of the cases which aroused the greatest furore concerned batsmen who fell to Larwood when the latter was setting an orthodox 6–3 field. This was the case with Bertie Oldfield, who admitted that he 'walked into it'. Most of the controversy was stoked up by Don Bradman – deservedly given a prominent place in your rogues' gallery – who simply could not stomach that his opponents had discovered a weakness in his armoury. If, on the other hand, it was the mere tactic of short-pitched bowling that caused you to cite Jardine, why did you not reserve any space for the West Indian bowlers who participated in the most disgraceful session international cricket has ever witnessed – at Old Trafford in 1976? And why was there no place for Brian Close and his despicable go-slow tactics that fraudulently earned Yorkshire the 1967 County Championship? And surely the fact that he has now met his maker should not blind us to the place which the utterly corrupt Hansie Cronje deserves in this list of cricketing lowlights?
**Walter Cairns,
via email**

THE TEN BIGGEST WASTES OF MONEY IN THE HISTORY OF FOOTBALL

*Current value of transfer fees calculated on the rate of inflation between then and now. Current costs calculated as a percentage of the record transfer fee, then and now.

01 STEVE DALEY Bought by Man City from Wolves in September 1979 for £1.43m. Today that is worth £4.3m and he would cost £28.1m.*

'Looking back it was a very foolish time,' Man City fan Nick Leeson told *OSM*. He's not talking about Barings, it's worse than that. He's recalling the era of casual spending which arguably set City back 20 years. That era is epitomised by Daley – 'the latest plutocratic passenger on the City gravy train' as the *Observer* described him – whose name remains a byword for big-money flops. The story goes that Malcolm Allison offered £400,000 and couldn't believe it when his chairman Peter Swales did the deal for a million more (Swales always denied it). Bryan Robson had recently joined Man United for a similar fee, so perhaps Daley was the victim of a perverse form of one-upmanship. The *Observer*'s report of his City debut reported that 'everything he did was neat and clever but none of it ever served to bind the side together'. It didn't get any better. Sold to Seattle Sounders in 1980 after 48 appearances (four goals).

02 RAFAEL SCHEIDT Bought by Celtic from Gremio in December 1999 for £4.8m. Today that is worth £4.9m and he would cost £9.8m.*

Stuart Slater, Tony Cascarino, Eyal Berkovic…Celtic could fill the whole list themselves, but the worst of a very bad lot is one of the most recent, Rafael Felipe Scheidt. When the John Barnes–Kenny Dalglish regime splashed out nearly five mill on a 23-year-old Brazilian international defender the Celtic faithful could be forgiven for thinking they'd made a spectacular signing. In a sense they had. Beset by injuries, and unable to settle, his form was terrible – 'The guy couldnae trap a bag of cement', one teammate remarked (his two caps came in friendlies). Even the club's understandable decision to put his first name on his shirt rebounded, upsetting his father. Scheidt started only one league game in the 1999/2000 season and was shipped out on loan by Martin O'Neill, apparently after being given the run-around in a friendly at Bray Wanderers. Loaned to Corinthians in 2000 after just three appearances.

03 GARRY BIRTLES Bought by Man Utd from Nottingham Forest in October 1980 for £1.25m. Today that is worth £3.2m and he would cost £23.8m.*

Yes, there was a time when United got it wrong. Very wrong, and Garry Birtles was the pick of the bunch. Yet in 1980 few people raised an eyebrow at the transfer when Dave Sexton gave Brian Clough so much for a player who in a couple of seasons at Forest had shown himself to be the epitome of the modern centre-forward: strong, mobile and deadly. But his loss of form at Old Trafford was shocking and mysterious – one match report described his performance as 'bordering on the statuesque'. He took almost an entire year (from 22 October 1980 until 19 September 1981) to break an embarrassing duck and finally score his first United goal. A predictable cut-price sale back to the City Ground ended a long nightmare. Sold for £300,000 to Nottingham Forest in 1982 after 63 appearances (12 goals).

04 RODNEY MARSH Bought by Man City from QPR in March 1972 for £200,000. Today that is worth £1.57m and he would cost £22.4m.*

When Marsh joined in March 1972, City were top of the league and apparently destined for the championship. Their side already boasted the likes of Francis Lee, Colin Bell and Mike Summerbee, but City boss Malcolm Allison thought Marsh was the missing piece in their jigsaw. City faded though, taking just eight points from their remaining eight games and finishing fourth, one point behind Derby's title-winners. Marsh, a special if self-indulgent talent, was blamed by many, among them his team-mate Neil Young. 'Rodney cost us the league, there's no doubt about it,' City's left-winger said. 'Whereas before we all knew where we were on the pitch and what we were doing, when Rodney came he unsettled the team. Somebody would give him the ball and I'd make a run ready to collect it in the box and it would never arrive. I'd turn around and he would be juggling it like a bloody seal.' Moved to Fulham on a free transfer in 1976 after 118 appearances (36 goals).

05 PETER MARINELLO Bought by Arsenal from Hibernian in January 1970 for £100,000. Today that is worth £9.2m and he would cost £14m.*

The Edinburgh-born winger with the face of a Bay City Roller was hailed at the time as the Scottish George Best. Now he is remembered as more of a Scottish Perry Groves. Marinello fulfilled the role of football's golden boy with relish (he modelled for Freeman's, appeared on *Top of the*

Pops with Pan's People, and starred in a poster campaign advertising milk) but flopped on the pitch. He made just one full appearance during the Double season of 1970/1 and scored only three goals in almost four seasons at Highbury. 'I squandered my talent,' he admitted years later. Sold for £100,000 to Portsmouth in 1973, after 32 appearances.

06 STAN COLLYMORE Bought by Aston Villa from Liverpool in May 1997 for £7m. Today that is worth £9.2m and he would cost £12.8m.*

Eyebrows that had been raised when Liverpool paid £8.5m for Collymore in 1995, were raised even further when Brian Little blew £7m to take Stan the Man to Villa Park after two disappointing seasons on Merseyside. Little gambled on the conceit that he could liberate the potential of British football's most infuriating talent. He couldn't, and seven months later resigned as Villa manager. Subsequent spells at Leicester, Bradford and Real Oviedo in Spain were brief and similarly abject. Sold for £500,000 to Leicester City in 1999 after 45 league appearances (seven goals).

07 GIANLUIGI LENTINI Bought by Milan from Torino in 1992 for £13m. Today that is worth £16m and he would cost £45.6m.*

The Italian Steve Daley, Lentini was a decent, but hardly world-beating winger whose fee, a world record, staggered everyone. The Vatican set the tone, condemning it as 'an offence against the dignity of work'. Milan, who were busy (and expensively) rebuilding as they tried to recreate the golden era of Gullit and Van Basten, were sorely disappointed with Lentini well before the car crash in 1993 which left him with a fractured skull and in a coma for 24 hours. He recovered but never again featured regularly in Milan's first team. Sold for £2m to Torino in 1997 after 63 appearances.

08 DENILSON Bought by Real Betis from São Paulo in July 1998 for £21.4m. Today that is worth £23.1m and he would cost £45.6m.*

A series of dazzling displays for Brazil at the friendly Tournoi in 1997 (a year ahead of France 98) prompted a stampede among Europe's big names for the 21-year-old left-winger, a stampede that was won – astonishingly – by a mediocre Spanish club offering a world-record fee. Betis had to wait a year for him to actually play for them, but his wildly inconsistent form did nothing to alter Betis's status as also-rans – he failed to score in 20 league games. (His finest hour in his first year was as the star of a series of Nike adverts to promote the 1998 World Cup.) His continuing travails have been badly received among the locals. 'Because I am not playing good football I don't want to go outside my house into Seville,' he said. Still at Real Betis.

09 LUTHER BLISSETT Bought by Milan from Watford in 1982 for £1m. Today that is worth £2.1m and he would cost £16m.*

Ninety-five league goals in just 246 appearances established Blissett as one of the most prolific strikers in Britain, thriving at Graham Taylor's no-nonsense Watford. Quite why Milan thought his robust talents would be similarly successful in Serie A remains one of football's enduring mysteries. He scored five goals in 30 games and, according to one Italian newspaper, was 'famous for missing open goals and for the inexorable precision with which he would find the goalpost'. His name lives on in Italy, however, but not for footballing reasons. 'Luther Blissett' has become a byword for anarchy. In 1997 four men went on trial in Rome for travelling on a train without tickets. When asked to identify themselves, all said they were Luther Blissett and argued that 'a collective identity does not need a ticket'. They explained that they chose Blissett because he was 'just a nice

Afro-Caribbean guy who had problems with the Italian way of playing football'. Sold back to Watford for £55,000 in 1984 after 30 appearances (five goals).

10 BRYN JONES Bought by Arsenal from Wolves in June 1938 for £14,000. Today that is worth £6.7m and he would cost £28.1m.*

'Arsenal have a big problem,' wrote the match reporter from the *Derby Evening Telegraph*, soon after Jones's move for a then world-record sum. 'Spending £14,000 on Bryn Jones has not brought the needed thrust into the attack. The little Welsh inside-left is clearly suffering from too much publicity, and is obviously worried. He is a nippy and quite useful inside-left, but his limitations are marked.' Derby won 2–1 at Highbury, and Arsenal went from champions to a disappointing fifth. Jones had dazzled at Wolverhampton Wanderers, where he was a huge crowd favourite, but his big-money move, deplored by MPs in the House of Commons, was not a success, particularly in his first season at the club (the war, of course, prevented him from making amends after that and cost him his best years as a player). 'No more money in the bank, what's to do about it? Let's put them to bed,' Arsenal fans sang about their team's big spending. Finished his Arsenal playing career in 1948.

READER RESPONSES

Things have changed quite a bit since Peter Marinello was bought by Arsenal for £100,000 in 1970. Peter was asked the question 'Where are you living now?' in an interview just after he had signed. The reply came: 'The club fixed me up with some smashing digs.

The landlady is fantastic and so is the house. Colour TV, the lot.' Oh, the sophistication of it all! **Michael McGuire, Co. Donegal**

01 DON BRADMAN is bowled for a duck in his final test innings, Australia v England, the Oval, 14 August 1948

It was always a shock of sorts when Bradman lost his wicket, so superlative was his batting, but the final dismissal of his Test career was the shock to beat them all. When the Don walked out to bat in Australia's first innings, he needed four runs to retire with the immortal average of more than 100. Given a standing ovation all the way to the wicket by the 30,000 crowd, and cheered by the English team, Bradman was then clean bowled for a duck second ball by an Eric Hollies googly. The gasps around the Oval were audible; cricket's ultimate perfectionist had been denied perfection in the final moment of his career at the crease. On returning to the pavilion, Bradman's reported reaction was a bemused 'Gee whizz, funny doing that.' The duck brought his average down to 99.94, although he could have yet made amends in Australia's second innings. But Ray Lindwall's pace bowling destroyed the English, who were crushed by an innings and 149 runs, and so Bradman never got his second chance.

02 JAMES 'BUSTER' DOUGLAS crushes Mike Tyson, Tokyo, 11 February 1990

Tyson entered 1990 with a record of 37 wins from 37 fights, with 33 of them coming by way of a knockout. No man (perhaps not even Muhammad Ali, some experts boldly said) could survive his blur of brutal uppercuts – least of all James 'Buster' Douglas, a 42–1 underdog. Tyson started slowly, but when, into the fifth and sixth rounds, Douglas was still connecting with decent shots, the half-empty Tokyo Dome had fallen eerily silent. Tyson then dropped Douglas with a right uppercut in the eighth – instantly it seemed that the champion's vulnerability had been an illusion – but Douglas survived, thanks to a long count. Two rounds later, though, Tyson was where he had never been before – on all fours, groping for his gumshield. Douglas had knocked out the 'baddest man on the planet'. 'If there was a Richter scale for sporting earthquakes,' Hugh McIlvanney wrote in the *Observer*, 'what happened would have to be considered two or three points clear of any other shock in twentieth-century boxing.'

03 JOHN DALY wins the 1991 US PGA title, Crooked Stick, Indianapolis, August 1991

Daly should never have even teed off. He was originally the tournament's ninth reserve but found himself pro-moted, on the eve of the first round, to first reserve after several players pulled out. Daly packed his clubs and drove through the night to reach the course – eight hours from his Memphis home – in the hope that he might yet sneak into the event. When he finally arrived in Indianapolis, a message left at his hotel informed Daly that Nick Price had withdrawn to attend the birth of his son. In Price's stead, and having borrowed the Zimbabwean's caddie, Daly (who hadn't even had time for a practice round) stormed to an astonishing three-shot victory with rounds of 69, 67, 69 and 71. 'I killed it,' he said afterwards. 'All four days, I didn't think. I just hit it. I just hit it so good, I had no fear out there…'

04 **ERIC CANTONA'S** kung fu kick, Selhurst Park, 25 January 1995

Cantona's horizontal assault on abusive Crystal Palace supporter Matthew Simmons – which earned the Frenchman an eight-month ban from football – remains one of the most gobsmacking incidents ever witnessed inside a British football stadium. Even before events at Selhurst Park, Cantona's hair-trigger temperament was well documented, but no one saw this coming. And this from a player who, in 1993, had said: 'Abroad the crowd is too far from the players. Here [in England] the game is warmer. There is even room for love between the crowd and players.'

05 **SIGNORINETTA** wins the Derby, Epsom, 1908

Signorinetta's 100–1 victory was the remarkable conclusion to an equine love story: the filly was owned and trained by Chevalier Ginistrelli, an Italian who had moved to England in the 1880s. Ginistrelli brought with him a small string of racehorses and subsequently bred Signorina, unbeaten in nine races as a two-year-old. After Signorina's racing career finished, she formed an attachment to a stallion named Chaleureux, who was led past Signorina's stable every morning on his way to the gallops. Ginistrelli became convinced that the two horses were in love – referring to the pair, he spoke of the 'boundless laws of sympathy and love – and fixed a mating. The product was Signorinetta, who became the 'darling of Chevalier's romantic heart'. As a two-year-old, Signorinetta showed no form, being unplaced in her first five races. Undaunted, the Italian prepared her for the Derby. There were 18 runners that year and only one horse started at longer odds than Signorinetta. Drawn 13, she took the lead halfway up the Epsom straight and won by two lengths, to become only the fourth filly to win the race (only three fillies have won since). Incredibly, two days later Signorinetta won the Oaks.

06 KEITH DELLER beats Eric Bristow, Embassy World Darts final, 1983

'He's not just an underdog, he's an underpuppy,' said Sid Waddell, commenting on 23-year-old Keith Deller's chances of beating Eric Bristow in the 1983 Embassy World Darts final. The unseeded Deller (reputedly the inspiration for the character Keith Talent, anti-hero of Martin Amis's novel *London Fields*) had reached the final against all odds and continued to defy form against Bristow. With the match poised at five sets each, and Deller one leg from victory, the Crafty Cockney made one of the less crafty decisions of his career – Bristow passed up the chance to go for bull's-eye and take the leg at that visit to the oche, believing Deller would never make his 138 outshot. Deller then nailed treble 20, treble 18 and double 12 to become world champion. 'I tell you,' shrieked Waddell, 'I've never seen anything like it in me life!'

07 CASSIUS CLAY beats Sonny Liston, Miami, 25 February 1964

Liston's reputation as an invincible ogre was well deserved, while Clay was considered a brash, if talented lunatic who had signed his own death warrant when he called the champion an 'ugly old bear'. Even before the contest had

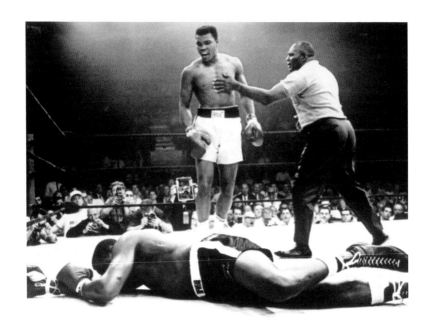

been set and Clay was being touted as a challenger, Liston had said: 'If they ever make the fight I'll be locked up for murder.' Clay's people had major doubts too. In the build-up to the fight, his doctor had studied maps, looking for the fastest possible route to the nearest hospital. But Clay, with his repeated promise to 'float like a butterfly and sting like a bee', had been telling the truth all along. He won the world heavyweight title at the age of 22 when a bleeding Sonny Liston, his left shoulder injured, was unable to answer the bell for the seventh round. Only three of 46 sports writers covering the fight had picked Clay to win. The new heavyweight champion of the world shouted down to them from the ring: 'Eat your words!'

08 MARGARET SMITH loses to Billie Jean Moffitt, Centre Court, Wimbledon, June 1962

No one gave the unseeded, bespectacled teenager from California a prayer; no one gave Margaret Smith's second-round opponent much thought at all. Moffitt had never even won a senior match at Wimbledon (she received a bye in the first round), while Smith, the No. 1 seed that year, was a formidable athlete who regularly trained and practised with men. And Moffitt would surely be overawed by having to play on Centre Court. So it seemed when Smith won the opening set easily, 6–1. But Moffitt quickly settled down and her dynamic play slowly began to unsettle Smith. Moffitt won the second set, 6–3, and held her nerve to win the match, taking the final set 7–5. 'I was in shock and I was actually crying for Margaret,' said Moffitt afterwards. 'A lot of people had bet a ton of money on her to win the tournament.'

09 HEREFORD beat Newcastle in the FA Cup Third Round, Edgar Street, 5 February 1972

Cue John Motson: 'Radford…now Tudor's gone down for Newcastle…Radford again…oh, what a goal! Radford the scorer, Ronnie Radford! And the crowd are invading the pitch…' No act of giant-killing defines the appeal of the FA Cup more than non-league Hereford's 2–1 defeat of First Division Newcastle in a third-round replay. Newcastle seemed certain to make it to the fourth round thanks to a late goal by Malcolm Macdonald, until Ronnie Radford's 30-yard screamer changed the game's momentum. Ricky George then bundled in a scrappy winner in extra time, prompting an even bigger pitch invasion, mostly by parka-clad teenagers. At the time, Hereford were the first non-league club to defeat a First Division side since 1949.

10 **MUNSTER** shut out the Mighty All Blacks, Limerick, 31 October 1978

A result which Irish playwright James Breen has described as 'the last great folk memory'. Breen was even moved to write a play, *Alone It Stands*, about Munster's proudest day. A record crowd of 13,000 turned up at Thomond Park to welcome Graham Mourie's fearsome All Blacks, who had reached Limerick unbeaten, with easy wins over Cambridge, Cardiff, West Wales and London Counties. But from the kick-off Munster tore into the visitors – the pattern for the game was set when New Zealand's Stu Wilson burst into the attacking line, only to be met with a crunching tackle from Munster's Seamus Dennison. Dennison was injured in the tackle but bravely continued. Munster took the lead in the ninth minute: Tony Ward lobbed a kick, Jimmy Bowen collected the bounce inside his own half, beat two men and fed Christie Cantillon for a try under the posts. A Ward drop goal saw Munster lead 9–0 at half-time. New Zealand roared back in the second half, but Munster's defence held. Ward's second drop goal, 11 minutes from time, crowned a 12–0 victory. Afterwards, Mourie said of Munster: 'They played the type of game we tried to play, but played it better.' It was the only match the All Blacks failed to win in 18 on the tour.

READER RESPONSES

You missed only one shock which I reckon should have made the top 10 - namely USA 1, England 0, at the 1950 World Cup.
Tony Potter,
via email

No Goran Ivanisevic winning Wimbledon? Surely that was a shock? Just ask Tim Henman. And it was a rather lovely one, too.
Robin Pharoah,
via email

01 UK AMERICAN FOOTBALL

First, there's the endless faux-American festivities that must be endured before a ball is kicked: every Scottish Claymores game, for example, begins with a 'spectacular fun time in the Party Zone – a themed entertainment extravaganza which has something for everyone'. Roughly translated, this means ex-Marillion singer Fish bellowing in front of a pipe band. Team names – Southend Sabres, Gateshead Senators, East Kilbride Pirates – are generally too embarrassing to shout aloud, while the game itself is an uneasy mix of the least interesting parts of rugby league and ITV's *Gladiators*. Only not nearly as much fun as that sounds.

02 CHESS

It may be the ultimate intellectual challenge, but as a live spectacle it lacks bite. The record for the longest mid-action pause belongs to Brazilian Francisco Trois, who pondered his seventh move against Luis Santos in 1980 for two hours and 20 minutes. That's a long time to be watching two socially awkward individuals sitting with their faces cupped in their hands. Enough time, indeed, to leave, watch a football match and return. The longest game between chess masters was a war of attrition between Ivan Nikolic and Goran Arsovic in Belgrade in 1989. It lasted over 20 hours. It was a draw. And neither kicked the other's shins under the table. Hopeless.

03 GOLF

If golf is indeed a good walk spoiled, what does that say about the people who pay for the privilege of plonking themselves behind the 18th green to watch a parade of identically dressed performers – 90 per cent of whom remain staunchly anonymous – play a few shots? The more adventurous souls who follow the glamour groups spend many miles and hours negotiating the immovable hazards of a 20-deep crowd of hollering toffs; dozens of self-important men in blazers clutching walkie-talkies; sand dunes; burger vans; and, if you're very unlucky, Alan Green whispering into a radio mike. Crucially, at the end of it all, you will still have no idea where the ball has gone.

04 SNOOKER

Perhaps it's the thought of Naseem Hamed cheering Ronnie O'Sullivan from the front row; perhaps it's the fact that other sporting world championships usually take place in some warm corner of the globe, whereas snooker forever belongs to a provincial theatre in Sheffield with the ghost of Alan Ayckbourn hanging in the air. Or perhaps it's simply because snooker is the quintessential TV sport, requiring crisps, cold drinks and conversation. If the 18.5 million TV viewers who watched Taylor beat Davis in 1985 had been required to sit in their living rooms in silence, stifling coughs and the urge to ask the person next to them to explain the re-spotting rule, most would have switched to *Minder* by the fourth frame.

05 RACE WALKING

Walking has been an Olympic event since 1908, yet it still looks like 20 desperate people racing to reach a single toilet cubicle. The distances covered – 20km, 50km – are difficult enough, but the main problem for spectators – aside from giggling – is detecting cheats. Walkers must have one foot touching the ground at all times, and TV replays frequently show them flouting this rule. However, for those watching on the streets it's impossible to tell – nobody wants to spend three hours cheering what appears to be a drunk Norman Wisdom impersonator only later to discover he's guilty of a two-foot violation. Walking scraped into the 2004 Olympics, but faces the axe in 2008. So be it.

06 SQUASH

The BBC commentator who remarked that squash is a poor spectator sport – comments made during the Beeb's squash highlights, natch – had a point. All the action takes place at the wrong end, and the ball – which is travelling at around 160mph – is roughly the size of a malnourished chestnut. World No. 17 Vicky Botwright captured the true concerns of squash fans when she expressed a desire to wear a thong during a recent British Open. Although she was eventually refused permission, Vicky realised that if you actively enjoy standing behind two extremely sweaty people as they charge about in tight sports gear, a well-executed drop-volley isn't necessarily uppermost in your mind.

07 TOUR DE FRANCE

Forget the cyclists, *Le Tour* is a dangerous enough ordeal for the spectators, especially as most don't have access to the kind of drugs favoured by many of the competitors. Two spectators have been killed in the past three years by Tour vehicles, and while it may seem like fun to amble along the banks of the Seine watching the opening stretch, to follow the whole event would mean a trek of nearly 3,500km, a fair proportion of which is a hellish ascent through the Alps and the Pyrenees. It also lasts for three weeks, a somewhat bigger commitment than travelling down the M1 to away games.

08 HOME NATION FOOTBALL FRIENDLIES

It's time for the home nations to offer free entry to friendlies, or else acknowledge that they're merely training exercises by playing them behind closed doors. When New Zealand visited Scotland in May 2003, 12,000 masochists paid good money to watch a team of semi-professionals who hadn't played football for a year – and that's just the current Scotland squad – toiling horribly at Tynecastle. In the 2003 friendly between England and Serbia, 43 different players – effectively four different teams – graced the pitch. As anyone who greets a brandished red card with glee will know, entertainment decreases in direct proportion to the amount of people involved in a game. Football, but not as we know it.

09 TENNIS: SPECIFICALLY, WIMBLEDON

Nothing against tennis as such, but the promise of some occasionally corking five-setters just isn't worth the candle. Two tickets for the men's final cost £2,500, while the vagaries of the English summer ensure that spectators spend the majority of their time sitting in the rain watching a plastic sheet being shuttled back and forth while they nibble the world's most expensive strawberries. If the thought of listening to Cliff Richard singing an a cappella medley of his hits doesn't make you physically unwell, or you like the idea of swapping neuroses with an endless parade of mad, bearded tennis dads, then all well and good. But be warned: you only get McEnroe on the telly.

10 CURLING

Essentially a mixture of bowls – only noisier, less relaxing and a good 20 degrees colder – and housework, nothing better illustrates how far Britain has fallen than the attempt to generate some 'curling fever' during the 2002 Winter Olympics. Using the GB team as the benchmark, all that appears to be on offer to the average fan is the sight of four comfortable-looking women talking on ice. Occasionally, one launches a huge circular stone and two more wield large brushes like crazed cleaners on overtime, while someone else yodels in an indeterminate language. Madness. One final fact: in Canada, more people watch curling than watch Premiership football in Britain. Case closed.

01 BORIS ONISCHENKO
The sword that scored on its own

Boris Onischenko, an army officer from Ukraine, entered the 1976 Olympics in Montreal a respected modern pentathlete who had won a silver medal in Munich four years earlier. He exited the Games in disgrace, with banner headlines around the world denouncing him as 'Disonischenko' and 'Boris the Cheat'.

Modern pentathlon is a five-discipline event that includes fencing, but Onischenko's épée was not the innocent weapon of competition it appeared. He had wired his sword so that he could trigger the electronic scoring system with his hand and register a hit at will.

The British team, who were to win the gold medal, were the first to suspect that Onischenko was up to something during his bout against Adrian Parker. When Jim Fox, Onischenko's next opponent, protested vehemently that his opponent was managing to score without hitting him, officials took away the Soviet athlete's sword. He continued with a replacement weapon, but soon afterwards news came through that he had been disqualified. Stories that he was later banished to the Siberian salt mines were probably exaggerated. The rules of the sport were changed, though, banning grips that could hide wires or switches.

02 CHICAGO WHITE SOX BASEBALL TEAM
Throwing the 1919 World Series

It became known as the Black Sox Scandal after eight Chicago White Sox were charged with accepting money from gamblers to throw the 1919 World Series, which was won 5–3 by the Cincinnati Reds. The gamblers, including former boxing champion Abe Attell, promised $100,000 to eight Sox players, and the following year a Chicago grand jury convened to investigate the case. Some of the

eight, including 'Shoeless' Joe Jackson, confessed to the jury. They had been told no action would be taken against them, but were immediately suspended. On their way out, a young boy is said to have called out to Jackson: 'Say it ain't so, Joe' (The phrase became one of the most famous in American sporting history, though Jackson later claims the incident never happened). In June 1921, just before the jury trial was due to begin, the players' testimony mysteriously disappeared and they were acquitted due to lack of evidence. But Kenesaw Mountain Landis, a former federal court judge who was installed as an all-powerful baseball commissioner, upheld the suspensions, declaring: 'Regardless of the verdict of juries…no player that sits in conference with a bunch of crooked players and gamblers…will ever play professional baseball.'

03 DIEGO MARADONA
The Hand of God

As the England goalkeeper Peter Shilton and the Argentine
captain Diego Maradona converged on Steve Hodge's
lofted backpass in the 52nd minute of their quarter-final at
the 1986 World Cup finals, the game's goalless scoreline
seemed secure. Maradona was, after all, a mere 5ft 4in,
eight inches shorter than Shilton, who reached out with his
right arm to punch the ball clear. Miraculously, or so it
seemed, the leaping Maradona managed to guide the ball
into the England net. Tunisian referee Ali Bennaceur, well
placed to spot any infringement, ignored the protests of
England's defenders that Maradona had handled the ball.
He didn't even bother to consult his Bulgarian linesman,
Bogdan Dotschev. But the slow-motion replay and, more
tellingly, a still picture taken by a Mexican photographer
showed that Maradona's left hand had deftly deflected
the ball home. 'It was partly the head of Maradona,' the
Argentine said the next day, 'and partly the hand of God.'
Later in the game Maradona scored a goal of unimpeach-
able brilliance as Argentina won 2–1 – and went on to win
the World Cup.

04 BEN JOHNSON
Awesome Olympic champion – until his drug test caught up with him

'I'd like to say my name is Benjamin Sinclair Johnson Jnr and this world record will last 50 years, maybe 100.' So said Ben Johnson after trimming four-hundredths of a second off the world record to finish first in the 100 metres at the Seoul Olympics in 1988. Within hours, though, his triumph was transmuting into one of the great Olympic scandals. In the Olympic Doping Control Centre, less than half a mile from where Johnson had received his gold medal, Dr Park Jong-Sei found that one of the numbered urine samples taken from the first four finishers contained stanozolol, a dangerous anabolic steroid. The number was Johnson's, confirming the suspicions of one American trainer, who had noted before the race that the Canadian's eyes were yellow, the result, he said, of 'his liver working overtime processing steroids'. Carl Lewis, Britain's Linford Christie and Calvin Smith were each promoted one place to fill the final medal positions as the disgraced Johnson, stripped of his gold, flew out of Seoul, feebly protesting his innocence. Johnson raced at the next Olympics after serving a two-year suspension, but was banned for life in 1993 after he tested positive again.

05 DAVID ROBERTSON
Transgressing golf's code of self-regulation

Golf prides itself on its culture of honesty and self-regulation, which makes the case of David Robertson, a former Scottish Boys champion, all the more remarkable. Robertson was playing in the final qualifying for the 1985 Open in Deal, Kent, and after 14 holes, his playing partners summoned an official and (according to a newspaper) 'after a long discussion Simmers [the official, Graeme] disqualified Robertson for not replacing his ball in the correct position on the green'. It was reckoned that, at times, he had moved his ball up to 20 feet. He did this by arriving at the green first, appearing to mark his ball, but merely picking it up and then carrying his marker on his putter around the green and dropping it much nearer the hole. He was fined £20,000 and banned for 20 years from playing as a pro by the PGA European Tour. The fine was never called in. Seven years later Robertson applied for and obtained his amateur status back and played in some amateur events in the Lothian region.

06 FRED LORZ
Marathon champion who travelled by car

The marathon at the St Louis Olympic Games of 1904 was held over a hilly course in the middle of a scorching afternoon. Small wonder only 14 of the 32 starters made it to the finish. First home, after three hours 13 minutes, was a New Yorker, Fred Lorz, who was immediately proclaimed the winner. He had already been photographed with Alice Roosevelt, the daughter of the President of the United States, and was about to be awarded the gold medal, when word got out that he had covered 11 miles as the passenger in a car. The crowd's acclaim rapidly turned to abuse. Although Lorz claimed it was a practical joke, he received a lifetime ban, which was later lifted. Thomas Hicks, an English-born American who was awarded the race, might have been disqualified himself after his handlers gave him strychnine and brandy to keep him going.

07 SYLVESTER CARMOUCHE
Jockey who ensured that punters didn't have the foggiest

On a foggy afternoon, a real pea-souper, in January 1990, Sylvester Carmouche surprised punters at Louisana's Delta Downs Racetrack by finishing first on 23–1 long-shot

Landing Officer. But all was not as it seemed. Carmouche had dropped out of the mile-long race while lost from view and then rejoined the field as they came round again before galloping to 'victory'. He should have waited a little longer. The fact that he won by 24 lengths and came within 1.2sec of the track record inevitably raised suspicions. The stewards disqualified him even though he protested his innocence. Later, he received a 10-year ban after the other jockeys in the race testified that Carmouche had not passed them. Eventually, he admitted to what he had done. He was reinstated after serving eight years of his suspension.

08 MICHEL POLLENTIER
Cyclist caught extracting the urine

Jacques Anquetil, one of the giants of the Tour de France, once remarked: 'You don't ride the Tour on mineral water.' Whatever it was Michel Pollentier rode it on we'll never be absolutely sure because he was disqualified during the 1978 race, not because of what was in his urine but because the urine he gave at a drug test wasn't his. Pollentier had just hurtled up the precipitous Alpe d'Huez to win, alone, and take the race leader's yellow jersey. According to one report, officials conducting the post-stage test became suspicious when 'Pollentier began pumping his elbow in and out as if playing a set of bagpipes'. Ordered to lift his jersey, the Belgian did so to reveal an elaborate plumbing system running from a rubber, urine-filled bulb under his arm to the test tube. Pollentier served a two-month suspension before he started racing again. The practice of substituting uncontaminated urine was reckoned to be widespread at the time.

09 THE SPANISH BASKETBALL TEAM
Faking disability at the 2000 Paralympic Games, Sydney

Officials of Spain's team resigned after a scandal involving mentally handicapped basketball players who, it transpired, had no mental disabilities. Journalist Carlos Ribagorda exposed the deception. He joined the team to break the story – and handed back his gold medal. According to Ribagorda, 15 athletes with no incapacity whatsoever were signed up by the Mentally Handicapped Sports Federation and told to pretend they were handicapped. The idea was to win more medals so the federation would qualify for extra funding. 'The only test they did was to make me do half a dozen sit-ups and take my blood pressure,' said Ribagorda. 'We never had any medical or psychological tests.'

10 MR MARTIN
The phantom horse race of 1898

A top-hatted gentleman calling himself Mr Martin walked into the offices of the *Sportsman* newspaper and asked them to publish the card of the Trodmore Hunt Steeplechase to be held in Cornwall on the August Bank Holiday Monday, 1898. The editor, impressed by the detailed programme of the event, agreed not only to print the card, but also to publish the results, which his new acquaintance would telegraph through. Had the editor checked, he would have discovered that Trodmore and its steeplechases did not exist. As it was, some fancy bets on Reaper to win the fourth race, which, according to the *Sportsman* it duly did at 5–1, had bookmakers paying out sizeable sums. Other bookmakers waited for the results printed in the *Sporting Life* the next day and here, because of a printer's error, Reaper's price was 5–2, which raised the alarm that this was a scam. No one was ever caught.

01 DEVON LOCH
falls in the 1956 Grand National

Two of Devon Loch's most fancied rivals, Must, the favourite, and Early Mist, the winner three years earlier, fell at the first, and with every stride the Queen Mother's horse appeared more dominant. Dick Francis, later to become a best-selling novelist, but on this afternoon Devon Loch's partner, fought to restrain the horse from going on too quickly. As they cleared the last and Francis kicked for home, the cheers for a royal victory thundered around the stands. 'Never had I felt such power in reserve,' Francis wrote later, 'such confidence in my mount, such calm in my mind.' Then, 55 yards from the line, disaster struck. The horse jumped slightly before collapsing on his stomach, legs thrust out in front and behind. The horse did manage to regain his feet but it was soon clear he could not carry on and ESB galloped past to win. None of the dramatic stories that have secured the Grand National's place in sporting legend has matched the mystifying subsidence of Devon Loch, whose name has become synonymous with sudden and inexplicable falls. Theories abound. That the horse tried to jump a shadow, was distracted by the crowd, had a cramp attack, suffered a blood clot on his hind leg and even that he was destabilised by breaking wind violently after his girth was made too tight at the start. Whatever the truth, it was one of the most sensational moments in sporting history.

02 MARY DECKER
trips over Zola Budd at the 1984 Olympics

Mary Decker, the outstanding female middle-distance runner of her generation, had hoped to run both the 1,500 and 3,000 metres at the Los Angeles Olympics in 1984 but withdrew from the 1,500 because the events overlapped. So her Olympic hopes were pinned on the longer race, in which her rivals included Zola Budd, the diminutive South African controversially granted British citizenship earlier in the year. Decker could have no idea what a dramatic effect her presence in the 3,000 metre final would have. At the 1,700-metre mark, the two bumped twice in the space of a few strides and Decker, tracking Budd, tripped on the British runner's right leg, her spikes digging deeply into Budd's heel. A dispirited Budd ran on, eventually limping home seventh, but Decker pitched forward on to the field, her race, and her only hope of a medal, over. Afterwards, a distraught Decker refused to accept Budd's apology.

03 NIGEL MANSELL'S
tyre bursts at the 1986 Australian Grand Prix

Virtually all Nigel Mansell had to do to win the drivers' championship was to keep going around the Adelaide street circuit. Entering the final race, he led Alain Prost by six points and Williams team-mate Nelson Piquet by seven. Well into the last third of the race, Mansell was second behind Keke Rosberg's McLaren, whose right rear tyre suddenly failed. Goodyear technicians tried desperately to inform the other Goodyear teams, including Williams, but as Mansell slipped into sixth gear and took off down the long Jack Brabham straight at close to 200mph his own left rear tyre exploded, showering the track with yellow, molten sparks. Prost sped by to win the world title by two points, while Mansell discovered later that if he had crashed into the wall on the straight, rather than expertly manoeuvre his stricken car into the escape road, the race would have been stopped and he would have been world champion.

04 DON FOX'S missed goal kick at the 1968 Rugby League Challenge cup final

He had already been named Man of the Match and now all Don Fox had to do was complete a triumphant afternoon for himself and Wakefield Trinity by knocking over the simplest of goal kicks. It was right in front of the posts and the points would overturn Leeds's 11–10 lead in the game's dying moments. But the Wakefield loose forward toe-poked it wide and sunk to his knees on the sodden Wembley turf. He never played again, nor has he spoken about the incident. But his older brother, Peter, the former Bradford, Featherstone and Great Britain coach, has explained: 'Although everyone else thought Wakefield had won the cup, I was worried because I could see our Don trying to wipe the ball on his jersey. But there wasn't a dry spot in the house. If I could I'd have gone on the field and let him wipe the ball on my shirt.'

05 OXFORD sink in the 1951 Boat Race

Crews have sunk before and since in the Boat Race, but this was the most remarkable of the calamities because of how soon the Oxford boat slipped beneath the Thames's choppy surface. As it turned out, Oxford's decision to choose the Surrey bank on winning the toss proved disastrous, exposing the crew to the full force of a strong westerly wind while Cambridge made quickly for the cover of the Middlesex bank. Water broke over the bows of the Oxford boat in the very first strokes and after a minute, reported *The Times*, 'it was all too plain to see that they must sink'. They did manage to stay afloat for two and a half minutes, but because they foundered before the end of the Fulham wall, the umpire decreed the race should be re-rowed the following Monday. This time, on a still day, Oxford reached the finish without mishap – 12 lengths behind Cambridge.

06 WILLIE SHOEMAKER
finishes too soon at the 1957 Kentucky Derby

The most successful jockey in history won four Kentucky Derbies but it is the Derby he didn't win that is as well remembered as his triumphs. Shoemaker held Gallant Man back early on, but eased through the nine-horse field coming into the straight, seeming to have the race at his mercy as he hit the front. But he mistook a trackside pole for the finish, stood up in the stirrups and after Iron Liege swept past him was unable to get going again to peg back the winner, who took the race by a nose. 'An error like that would have destroyed most men,' said Shoemaker's great rival, Eddie Arcaro, who finished fourth on Bold Ruler. 'Only a guy like Willie could have survived it. He's a tough sonofagun.'

07 JIM PETERS collapses during the
1954 Empire Games marathon

British marathon runner Jim Peters set four world records between 1952 and 1954, lowering it from 2hr 25min 39sec to 2hr 17min 40sec. Victory in the 1954 Empire Games in Vancouver seemed a formality, even more so when in the race itself he opened a lead of more than three miles and entered the stadium 20 minutes ahead of his closest rival. But, having run the entire race on a scorching day without drinking any water, he fell repeatedly and then started to crawl on the track. His team-mates, including Roger Bannister, felt powerless to help him, remembering Dorando Pietr's disqualification in the 1908 Olympic marathon after being helped across the line. He was eventually rescued when it became clear he was not going to finish. In the medical centre, he asked if he had won. 'You did very well,' said a nurse.

08 JEAN VAN DE VELDE'S
final hole disaster at the 1999 Open

Jean Van de Velde looked invincible as he stood on the final tee at Carnoustie holding a three-shot lead. A few minutes later, the 33-year-old Frenchman was rolling up his trousers to wade into Barry Burn where his ball lay under water. That was after his first shot landed on the 17th fairway and his second, having struck a stand and a rock, ended in heavy rough. His third plopped into the burn, his fourth was a drop, his fifth disappeared in to a bunker, his sixth rolled on to the green and his seventh, a putt from seven feet, found the centre of the hole. Van de Velde then finished last in a three-way play-off for the title with winner Paul Lawrie and Justin Leonard.

09 US SPRINTERS'
no-show at the 1972 Olympics

Eddie Hart and Rey Robinson had both been timed at 9.9sec in the US trials and were regarded as the only men capable of beating the great Russian Valery Borzov. All three won their first-round heats in the morning, but there was no sign of Hart or Robinson as the 4.15pm start time approached for the second round. Their coach, Stan Wright, working from an 18-month-old preliminary schedule, thought their races were at 7pm and Robinson was just leaving the village three-quarters of a mile from the track when he saw on an ABC-TV monitor the very heat in which he was supposed to be running. Only the third and least fancied American, Robert Taylor, arrived in time for his heat. He went on to finish second in the final behind Borzov, who won the gold in 10.14sec.

10 LEEDS GOALKEEPER GARY SPRAKE

throws the ball into his own net

If the great Leeds United teams of the late sixties and early seventies had a weak leak it was their Welsh international goalkeeper, Gary Sprake, a custodian capable of making a breathtaking save one moment and a slapstick error the next. His attempt to save Peter Houseman's shot in the 1970 FA Cup final, which ended in the net when Sprake dived over the ball, was viewed by millions of television viewers, but the mistake that caused him the greatest embarrassment came in a League match against Liverpool at Anfield on a wet December afternoon in 1967. Just before half-time, and with Leeds trailing 1–0 to a Roger Hunt goal, Sprake safely gathered the ball as a Liverpool attack broke down. But as he went to throw the ball out, he seemed to change his mind, and in trying to check his action mid-throw he merely succeeded in releasing the ball behind him and into his own net. The DJ on duty at Anfield that day found the perfect record to play during the half-time interval, Des O'Connor's 'Careless Hands', a best-selling song at the time. In fact, they charitably played it every time Sprake came back.

READER RESPONSES

While it is difficult to disagree with many of the choices made by your good selves I believe there is one glaring omission. Surely David Seaman being beaten by a speculative punt from the halfway line in the last minute of the Cup-Winners Cup final in 1994 must be in there somewhere? As an Arsenal fan I'm not sure if the fact that the scorer (Nayim) was an ex-Tottenham player makes it better or worse.
**Keith Batten,
via email**

THE UGLY

01 RONALDO

Faux pas: patronising 1.8 billion Orientals
with a Jim Davidson-inspired schoolyard gag

When the world's most famous footballer flew into South Korea last May to prepare for the World Cup he was still struggling to regain his reputation. Cursed by injury and poor form since his dramatic collapse at the 1998 World Cup final in Paris, the fêted Brazilian striker had slowly dragged himself back into the international reckoning, with a clutch of well-timed goals in World Cup warm-up games. Yet he was still a 20–1 outsider to be tournament top scorer. By the time he pulled this childish stunt on arrival at Kimhae airport, however, it's unlikely you could have got 1000–1 on him leaving the country alive. Still, the two-strong welcoming party enjoyed the gag.

02 PIERRE VAN HOOIJDONK

Faux pas: casually insulting the poverty-stricken and dispossessed

Buck-toothed, black and with a tidy right foot, Pierre was Holland's prototype Ronaldo, albeit without the flair for Far Eastern politics. Still, at least the Brazilian's clumsy attempts at mediation were delivered with a certain amount of grace and humour (however misplaced), concepts alien to the dunderhead Dutchman. In 1996, the freescoring Van Hooijdonk was negotiating his contract with Celtic, confident that his goals for the Glasgow club would be rewarded with a generous new pay packet. Manager Tommy Burns pulled out all the stops for his star player offering Pierre a £7,000 a week rise, a princely sum at the time, particularly from a club with a reputation for counting the pennies. But the offer didn't impress Pierre much. 'It may be good enough for the homeless,' he sulked, 'but not for an international striker.' Van Hooijdonk was offloaded to Nottingham Forest in 1997 and Feyenoord in 2002 where he continues to enchant team-mates and fans alike with his modesty and wit.

03 FUZZY ZOELLER

Faux pas: racially abusing the world's best golfer

An epoch-making moment in the history of professional golf, the 1997 US Masters made sporting history on several fronts. It was the first time Tiger Woods won a major championship, a feat he achieved with some ease, beating his nearest rival by a record 12 shots. It was significant, too, because it witnessed a black golfer donning the green jacket for the first time. But, perhaps above all, the 1997 US Masters was made infamous by the imbecilic rantings of veteran American tour pro and Dean Martin lookalike Fuzzy Zoeller. Teeing himself up nicely with a patronising swipe at the 21-year-old Woods – or 'that little boy' as the

Fuzz preferred to call him – Zoeller saved his oratorial tour de force for the climax of the tournament. Remarking on the Masters tradition for allowing the winner to choose the menu at the following year's Champions dinner, Zoeller said that he hoped Woods, by then coasting to victory, 'wouldn't serve fried chicken, or collared greens, or whatever the hell they serve'. Fuzzy later apologised to Woods, but the slip – which he claimed was just a 'joke' – cost him a major sponsorship deal and made his life 'total hell'. Shame.

04 RICHARD KRAJICEK
Faux pas: suggesting, a tad indelicately,
that women tennis players are 'lazy, fat pigs'

Perhaps it was the heat that summer or maybe he simply poured too much cream on his strawberries, but something was definitely eating Richard Krajicek in July 1992. 'Eighty per cent of the women playing at Wimbledon are lazy, fat pigs and shouldn't be allowed on the show courts,' he raged on Dutch radio. To be fair, when challenged the next day on this seemingly unprovoked attack Krajicek relented. 'I said 80 per cent of the top 100 are fat pigs but I just over-exaggerated a little bit. What I meant was only 75 per cent.' A qualification which cleared things up nicely.

05 JOHN ROCKER
Faux pas: vicious and ugly sideswipe at virtually
all US immigrants and Aids victims

It was during an otherwise innocuous *Sports Illustrated* interview in 1999 that the Atlanta Braves relief pitcher – a man who had clearly never heard Michael Owen flat-batting a succession of probing questions – betrayed his own particularly vicious brand of xenophobia. Rocker stated that he would never join a New York team because he wouldn't want to ride a subway train 'next to some queer with Aids'. Warming to his theme, he went on: 'The biggest thing I don't like about New York are the foreigners. I'm not a very big fan of foreigners. You can walk an entire block in Times Square and not hear anybody speaking English. Asians and Koreans and Vietnamese and Indians and Russians and Spanish people and everything up there. How the hell did they get into this country?' 'They' might well ask the same of you, Mr Rocker.

06 DALEY THOMPSON
Faux pas: assorted, at the 1984 Olympic Games
Thompson's appearance in LA was one strange, extended masterclass in idiocy. The decathlon champion whistled the British national anthem and then flounced into a press conference wearing a T-shirt which asked the question: 'Is the World's 2nd Greatest Athlete Gay?' He meant Carl Lewis, but then again there's no accounting for the judgement of a man who also expressed a desire to reproduce with Princess Anne.

07 GRAEME SOUNESS
Faux pas: flag-planting in Turkey
Yes, it's a questionable inclusion but, as any Celtic or Everton fan will tell you, Souness has rarely set out to annoy a

rival without giving it at least three weeks' serious prior thought. So, for the sheer nerve and bloody-mindedness of the act (and because he claims to have acted spontaneously), Souness is in. The venue was Fenerbahce's Saracoglu stadium, a ground with more flares than a Showaddywaddy convention. The game? A Turkish Cup final in 1996 between the hosts and their hated rivals, Galatasaray, then managed by the moustachioed Scot. Having watched his team triumph 2–1, Souness decided to celebrate by planting a 15-foot high Galatasaray flag slap bang in the middle of the Fenerbahce pitch. He survived, but only just.

08 MARTINA HINGIS

Faux pas: failing to wash out her mouth with soap and water

Another tennis player, another bizarre press-conference outburst. During the 1999 Australian Open, Hingis was reported to have told German and Swiss journalists that the French player Amelie Mauresmo, whom she would later face in the final, 'travels with her girlfriend – she is half a man'. Offensive? Yes. Odd? Undoubtedly. But a comment not entirely without precedent. Previous to this slur, Hingis had informed an American magazine that the Chilean player Marcelo Rios 'looks like he lives in the forest'. Tickets are reportedly still available for Martina's upcoming retirement party.

09 IVICA KOSTELIC

Faux pas: bringing Adolf Hitler back into off-piste conversation

The 23-year-old Croatian skier may have mastered the snowy mountains of Europe, but he's stuck firmly on the nursery slopes of life when it comes to the art of diplomacy. Kostelic landed himself in hot water in January this year when he was asked by the Croatian newspaper *Nacional* how it felt to stand on top of the slope about to burst into action. 'I feel powerful, all-conquering, like a German soldier ready for battle in 1941,' Kostelic said. Given that, the previous summer in conversation with a reporter on the same paper, Kostelic had talked in awed tones about the scale of the Luftwaffe attack on Britain in 1940, and favourably compared Hitler to other world leaders of the time (unlike Stalin, Hitler killed only those who crossed him, he suggested), the general feeling was that Ivica might be harbouring somewhat right-leaning sympathies. His father, however, had a truly compelling counter-argument. 'Ivica cannot possibly be a Nazi,' he said. 'He's a Catholic.'

10 AUSTIN HEALEY
Faux pas: putting the wind up the Aussies

Big mouth, big head, precious little brain. Austin Healey's Diary comments during the 2001 Lions tour of Australia ultimately backfired on him when he failed to match his bombastic words with action. Orchestrating a one-man campaign against the Aussies from the safe harbour of his newspaper column was rather like a child blowing raspberries at passers-by from the back seat of his parents' speeding car. Having pathetically nicknamed the local press 'the Sydney Morning Sun Telegraph Herald Load of Shite', Healey directed the full force of his satirical muscle towards the Wallabies lock forward Justin Harrison as the final and decisive Test loomed. He derided Harrison as 'plod', 'plank' and 'the ape Harrison' before asking cockily, 'Do you think one of us will have the final say? I'll say so.' Australia, whose starting line-up included the 'plank', won the Test and the series. 'Plod' also stopped a match-winning Lions try at the death. Doh!

01 FISCHER V SPASSKY
Chess (1970-2)

The ultimate sporting metaphor. The early seventies may not quite have been the height of the Cold War, but the atmosphere between the two superpowers was still icy. The virulently anti-communist Richard Nixon was in the White House, Brezhnev in the Kremlin and the arms race was in fearsome, full flow. And then there was the chess. Soviet dominance of the world's most cerebral game (35,000 players in the States, four million across the Soviet Union) was suddenly threatened by Bobby Fischer (*pictured*), a deeply eccentric 29-year-old from Chicago who in 1972 became the first player from outside the Soviet Union to challenge for the title of world chess champion. The holder was Boris Spassky. Fischer almost refused to travel to

Iceland, until US Secretary of State Henry Kissinger called and appealed to his patriotism. 'I have been chosen to teach the Russians some humility,' Fischer declared.

And the winner was Fischer, by 12½–8½ when Spassky resigned in the last game, two months after the contest began. The mysterious and paranoid Fischer never defended his title.

02 INDIA V PAKISTAN
Cricket (1952 onwards)

Since the creation of Pakistan by the Partition of India in 1947, cricket on the subcontinent has been riven by tensions and an awesome rivalry, albeit one continually overshadowed by politics. Perhaps the most dramatic match was in 1999 when, with India on the brink of defeat, the 65,000 crowd at Eden Gardens in Calcutta invaded the pitch and caused a three-hour delay. The match, eventually won by Pakistan, was completed in total silence in an empty stadium.

And the winners are Pakistan. In just 12 series (and 47 Tests) over 50 years they lead 4-2, and 9-5 in matches. The likeliest result, though, is a draw: there have been 33.

03 ROBINSON V LA MOTTA
Boxing (1942–51)

The rivalry immortalised in the film *Raging Bull* was boxing's finest. Sugar Ray Robinson and Jake La Motta slugged it out over nine years, six fights and 65 rounds of brutal middleweight boxing. Every fight went the distance (La Motta became the first man to beat Robinson in their second clash in 1943) until their final meeting in Chicago Stadium on 14 February 1951 when 13 savage rounds into the 'St Valentine's Day Massacre' Robinson finally knocked out La Motta. 'I fought Sugar Ray so many times I've got sugar diabetes,' La Motta later remarked.

And the winner was Robinson, who won five of the six fights.

04 BORG V MCENROE
Tennis (1978-81)

Tennis has thrown up more than its fair share of compelling rivalries, but none compares with this perfect contrast of talent and temperament. Björn Borg: brilliant baseliner, cool Swede, unflappable and sexy. John McEnroe: sublime volleyer, brash New Yorker, volatile. For three years their rivalry transcended tennis. It was defined by their unforgettable fourth-set tie-break in the 1980 Wimbledon final. With appropriate irony, McEnroe won it 18–16, but lost the title in the next set. A year later he ended Borg's streak of five Wimbledon titles, and a few months after that the Swede retired – a rivalry cut off in its prime. McEnroe says his professional life was never so much fun again.

And the winner was No one: they tied at 7-7 - but McEnroe won three of their four grand slam finals.

05 CELTIC V RANGERS
Football (1891 onwards)

The greatest footballing rivalry of them all because of its scalding passion. The sectarianism that underpins it is vile, but the occasions it invariably produces are sport at its rawest.

And the winners are Rangers, by a surprisingly large margin: 238-138, with 136 draws.

06 NAVRATILOVA V EVERT
Tennis (1975-88)

If Borg v McEnroe was brief but glorious, this was protracted and nearly as good. Again there was the contrast in styles, but this time between two players who dominated for more than a decade – between them the pair won 18 out of the 19 slams between 1982 and 1986.

And the winner was Navratilova, who had an overall lead of 15, and won 10 of their 14 grand slam finals.

07 AMERICA V EUROPE
Ryder Cup golf (1979 onwards)

America routinely thrashed Great Britain and Ireland, but the creation of a European side has led to a heady mix of courage, patriotism, sportsmanship, gamesmanship, drama, awful outfits and strange dance steps. Plus an indecent amount of brilliant golf.

And the winner is The US edge it 6-5, with one tie.

08 PROST V SENNA
Formula One (1984-94)

How Formula One today could do with a rivalry as bitter and compelling as this one. Two of the greatest drivers of all time, pitted repeatedly against one another. Stylistically they were different, but essentially it was personal. 'Metaphorically,' Prost reflected, 'Senna wanted to destroy me.' The enmity peaked in 1989 when the pair forced each other off the track at Suzuka. Senna (behind in the championship and needing to finish ahead of Prost) tried to dive past the Frenchman at a tight chicane only for their McLarens to lock wheels and exit the track. Senna rejoined to win the race but was disqualified for a rule infringement. The championship was effectively over…as was any chance of the pair being reconciled.

And the winner was Prost, just. In the 116 times they raced the Frenchman finished ahead of Senna 54 times (Senna ahead of Prost 50 times, with neither finishing in 12 races) and he also won four championships to the Brazilian's three.

09 USOVA and ZHULIN V GRISCHUK and PLATOV
Ice Skating (1992-4)

At the Albertville Olympics in 1992 the Russian pairs came third and fourth in the ice dance, but this was purely a precursor to another kind of rivalry. Usova and Zhulin were an item, Grischuk and Platov were not. After the Olympics,

Usova walked into Spago's restaurant in Hollywood, caught her husband sharing a cocktail with Grischuk, and promptly punched her rival in the face. Two years later, at the Lillehammer Games, Grischuk and Platov won gold to their rivals' silver. Usova refused to go to the medallists' press conference and she and Zhulin subsequently broke up.

And the winner was Ice dancing, which got a lot of publicity.

10 ALEX HIGGINS V REST OF THE WORLD
(1971 onwards)

Seventeen arrests, one (so-far) successful battle with throat cancer, a lifelong hostility towards taxi drivers and bar staff, two marriages, five fights with fellow professionals, one stabbing, five suspensions, two suicide attempts, one ban from *Pot Black*, one petition for bankruptcy, 15 bans from snooker's governing body, one enduring feud with Dennis Taylor, bans from just about every hotel in Greater Manchester, several forests' worth of tabloid stories… And, incidentally, two World Snooker championships, in 1972 and 1982.

And the winner is The public, who have watched, bemused and amused by the whole soap opera.

**THE TEN
BIGGEST
CHOKES
IN THE
HISTORY
OF SPORT**

01 GREG NORMAN
The Masters, Augusta, 1996

In the opening round of the 1996 Masters Greg Norman shot a course-record 63. Three days later he contrived to go round the same 18 holes at Augusta National in 15 strokes more. In the process he blew a six-shot lead – the biggest in Masters history – over Nick Faldo and converted it into a five-shot deficit. On the day Faldo was brilliant, but brilliance alone would not have been enough to catch the Great White Shark had Norman not folded and run up a Great White flag.

02 JANA NOVOTNA
Wimbledon final, 1993

Novotna led Steffi Graf 6–7 6–1 4–1 and at 40–30 in the sixth game of the deciding set had a service point for a 5–1 lead over the German. But Novotna double-faulted and arguably the greatest disintegration in a Wimbledon final had begun. Not much more than 10 minutes later Graf had won 7–6 1–6 6–4. The Duchess of Kent, trying to console the Czech player at the awards ceremony, said: 'Don't worry, Jana, you'll be back next year.' That did it for Novotna – 'I wanted to handle myself well,' she said, 'but when she smiled at me I just let go' – who wept uncontrollably on the Duchess's shoulder.

03 ENGLAND PENALTY TAKERS
Turin 1990, Wembley 1996, St Etienne 1998
The roll-call of shame. Step forward Stuart Pearce, Chris Waddle, Gareth Southgate, Paul Ince and David Batty. Put England up against it, a semi-final of a major competition for example. Have them play against a top team and they will excel. They will overcome deficits, tears, near-misses and red cards. After 120 minutes of thrilling football the two teams can't be separated except by a penalty shoot-out. And then it happens. Someone has to miss, fail, be cast as the goat. But why does it have to be a man with three lions on his shirt who finds the task of kicking a ball into a goal from 12 yards so bloody difficult?

04 DAVID BEDFORD
Olympic 5,000m, 1972

Between the end of the Australian Ron Clarke's reign and the start of the Africans' domination, David Bedford was among the most feared track athletes over longer distances. At the 1972 Games, the Briton ran disappointingly in the 10,000m to finish sixth but had the chance to make amends in the 5,000m. He was ranked number one in the world and had recently come within a second of Clarke's world record. A naturally aggressive front runner, Bedford seemed to have the race set up for him when it settled into a slow, tactical contest. But after four laps, the point at which he was due to move ahead, Bedford, who seemed weighed down by expectations, lost heart and finished anonymously down the field.

05 ROBERT DURAN
World title fight, New Orleans, 1980

When they choke, most athletes prefer that no one notices, that the world sees it as a defeat unbesmirched by an inner surrender. Robert Duran, the fearsome Panamanian boxer, usually did things differently – and in his welterweight title fight against Sugar Ray Leonard in New Orleans in 1980 he performed one of the most unashamed and conspicuous chokes of all time. Confused and exasperated by Leonard's slick movement, Duran suddenly stopped fighting in the eighth and declared, '*No mas, no mas.*' He couldn't take any more and didn't mind who knew it.

06 DOUG SANDERS
Open Championship, St Andrews, 1970

Doug Sanders had two putts from 30 feet to win the 1970 Open at St Andrews, edging out the mighty Jack Nicklaus in the process. Sanders left his first effort – downhill and across the green – 30 inches short. Then things went really wrong. 'I was confident standing over it, and then I saw what I thought was a little piece of sand on my line,' recalls Sanders. 'Without moving my feet, I bent down to pick it up, but it was a piece of grass. I didn't take time to move away and get reorganised. I mishit the ball and pushed it to the right of the hole. It was the most expensive missed putt in the history of the game.' Too true. The following day he lost the 18-hole play-off to Nicklaus by a stroke.

07 JIMMY WHITE
World snooker final, Sheffield, 1994

This would surely be Jimmy White's year. The Whirlwind had lost in five world finals – including the first four of the 1990s – but now, in the tightest of showdowns against his nemesis Stephen Hendry, victory was just a few pots away. A 75 clearance by White had taken the score to 17–17 and in the deciding frame he had a straightforward black off the spot to put the championship beyond Hendry's reach. 'It was a bread-and-butter pot for someone of Jimmy's class,' said one veteran observer, 'but he missed it by so much that it could only have been a choke.'

08 GAVIN HASTINGS
Rugby World Cup, Murrayfield, 1991

It should have been as straightforward as turning off a light switch for Scotland's Mr Reliable, Gavin Hastings. But in a World Cup semi-final against England – in front of your home crowd – a penalty from in front of the posts can unsettle even those with the iciest blood in their veins. Sure enough, Hastings sliced it and the score remained 6–6 until Rob Andrew's drop goal nicked it for England. As Hastings's kick sailed wide, the normally restrained England winger Rory Underwood let slip a four-letter expletive in surprise. That's how big a shock it was.

09 SCOTT BOSWELL Cheltenham & Gloucester Trophy final, Lord's, 2001

Two overs costing 23 runs isn't that rare in one-day cricket but when they consist of nine wides – eight in the second over, including five on the bounce – then it is a rare feat indeed. Scott Boswell had been man of the match when Leicestershire beat Lancashire in the semi-final, so it was no surprise when he was selected ahead of Devon Malcolm for the Lord's showpiece against Somerset. But under the pressure that comes with a major final Boswell's chest-on, round-arm action disintegrated and Somerset cruised to victory. A month later Boswell was released from his contract.

10 SCOTT NORWOOD Super Bowl XXV, Tampa, 1991

In suburban Virginia, Scott Norwood sells insurance. Those of his clients who recognise his name don't think of him as an ex-All Pro kicker in the NFL, they think of a 47-yard field goal that sailed 'wide right' in the dying seconds of Super Bowl XXV. Norwood's Buffalo Bills went into the 1991 Super Bowl as seven-point favourites over the New York Giants but with eight seconds left they trailed 20–19. Norwood had the chance to win it all but his kick drifted past the right upright. Within a year he was out of the game.

READER RESPONSES

Any list of chokes surely has to have room for Scott Hoch (nickname 'Hoch the Choke'), the American golfer who has made a career out of snatching defeat from the jaws of victory. There's lots to pick from but I'd settle for the two-footer he missed in 1989 to give Faldo his first Masters. Delicious!
Ken Crosslan,
via email

What about Gordon Smith's miss at the end of the 1983 FA Cup final when Brighton were drawing 2-2 with Manchester United? The miss gave Brighton fanzine the title *And Smith Must Score*.
Paul Harrop,
Maidstone

01 FRANK WORTHINGTON (1972)

Vital ingredients: Swedish girls, a move to Liverpool, an excess of sexual activity

The seventies were football's sixties – an era of promiscuous abandon – but even in those days Frank Worthington was a special talent. A notorious womaniser, the breakdown of his move to Liverpool in 1972 is one of the game's enduring urban legends. Having all but signed, the deal fell through because he failed a medical. The rumour was that he had a dose of the clap. In fact, he had high blood pressure – but that was brought on by excessive sexual activity. Bill Shankly told him to have a break, and return for a second medical. Worthington went to Majorca, continued his lifestyle and failed the medical again.

02 PETER SHILTON (1980)

Vital ingredients: booze, infidelity in a quiet country lane

Shilton was arrested for drink-driving after being found at 5am in a country lane with a woman called Tina in his car. When Tina's husband Colin arrived he said the pair were partially clothed. Shilton hurriedly drove away and crashed into a lamp-post. He admitted 'taking a lady for a meal' and was fined £350 and banned from driving for 15 months. He then had to endure countless terrace chants of 'Shilton, Shilton, does your missus know you're here?'

03 PETER BEAGRIE (1991)

Vital ingredients: booze, a motorcycle, a plate-glass window

While on Everton's 1991 pre-season tour of Spain, Beagrie went on a boozy night out following a game with Real Sociedad. In the early hours he flagged down a Spanish motorcyclist who gave him a lift home. Upon arriving at his hotel he couldn't wake the night porter, so Beagrie commandeered the bemused Spaniard's bike, rode it up the hotel steps and straight through a plate-glass window. Only it was the wrong hotel. Beagrie required 50 stitches.

04 DON HUTCHISON (1996)

Vital ingredients: booze, a Budweiser label, a bad tackle

While on holiday in Ayia Napa in 1994, an inebriated Hutchison hid his wedding tackle behind a Budweiser label. When a bystander's snaps appeared in the tabloids, his manager at Liverpool Roy Evans declared: 'If Hutchison is flashing his **** again that's out of order.' Hutchison had form. A year earlier he had spotted female students videoing their graduation celebrations in a wine bar, unzipped his flies and announced, 'Zoom in on this!' After the Ayia Napa incident he was fined £5,000, dropped, transfer-listed – and eventually shipped off to West Ham (where he was known to fans and team-mates as 'Budweiser').

05 GEORGE BEST (1970)

Vital ingredients: football's best-known stud, an impending FA Cup semi-final

In terms of attracting women, Best even put Frank Worthington in the shade. His most notorious moment came when he was caught in flagrante delicto by his manager Wilf McGuinness at the team's hotel on the afternoon of Man Utd's FA Cup semi-final against Leeds in 1970. Best had chatted up the woman on the hotel's stairs. McGuinness wanted to send him home, and only the intervention of Sir Matt Busby enabled Best to play. 'He had an absolute nightmare,' McGuinness recalled. 'We drew 0–0 again, and George had the chance to win it, but fell over the ball in front of goal.'

06 ALAN SHEARER (1997)

Vital ingredients: booze, a national hero, Keith Gillespie sprawled on the ground

Newcastle's players went out on the town during a break in Dublin in 1997, a frolic that culminated in Phillipe Albert wearing a traffic cone on his head. Gillespie, meanwhile, was flicking bottle tops at Shearer. 'Al was saying, "Do that one more time and I'll give you a good hiding,"' David Batty revealed in his autobiography. The pair went outside and then Batty saw a pair of legs in the air. 'We ran out to see Gillespie spark out in the gutter. There was blood everywhere. Allegedly, Keith had taken a swing as the two made their way towards the rear of the pub and Al had turned and decked him.'

07 DWIGHT YORKE (with guest appearance from MARK BOSNICH, 1998)

Vital ingredients: four girls, a hidden video, dressing up in women's clothing

Dwight Yorke's nocturnal activities in Manchester attracted the displeasure of his manager Alex Ferguson on a number of occasions. His most notorious moment came when he secretly videoed a drink-fuelled sex romp involving himself, the then Villa keeper Mark Bosnich and four girls at his luxury house in Sutton Coldfield. The video showed Yorke and Bosnich giving thumbs-ups to the secret camera and wearing women's clothing. Yorke later threw the video out with his rubbish, but unfortunately for him a '*Sun* reader' found it and the pictures were then shared with a disbelieving nation.

08 JODY MORRIS (2001)

Vital ingredients: the Chelsea Four, nightclubs

Just when you thought footballers were beginning to learn how to behave themselves, Chelsea produce a youngster from another era. The Chelsea Four (Morris, plus Frank Lampard, John Terry and Eidur Gudjohnsen) spent the day after the World Trade Center atrocity getting drunk in front of grieving Americans in a Heathrow hotel. A month later Morris was involved in a nightclub fight. And he has form: including spending a night in the cells after being arrested for being drunk and disorderly after a binge in Wimbledon last year. Morris and pals were reported to police for fighting in a pub and lying in the road with their tops off.

09 ALLY MCCOIST (2001)

Vital ingredients: Patsy Kensit, an air hostess

It may come as a surprise to have a second entrant from 2001, but like Jody Morris McCoist's remarkably bad behaviour could not be ignored. Not content with his affair

with Patsy Kensit (an affair that he brought to an end, which made all the papers) it then transpired he didn't have one mistress but two. The second was 28-year-old air hostess Donna Gilbin, who didn't know about Patsy and was sure Patsy didn't know about her. 'He was a wonderful lover and he made me melt,' Donna told the *People*. 'But now I know that he's just a liar and a hypocrite. My world fell apart when the bombshell dropped.'

10 TOMMY TYNAN (1991)
Vital ingredients: booze, the game 'buzz', a kettle (used as a weapon)

As the Torquay team attempted to bond before the 1991 play-offs, a session of the drinking game 'buzz' was organised. When Tynan tried to break up an argument between his captain Wes Saunders and player-coach Russell Musker, Saunders punched Tynan, leaving him with a cut eye. The players then went to bed, but at 2am Tynan went to Saunders's room to seek vengeance and, according to chairman Mike Bateson, 'he picked up the nearest thing handy, which was a kettle, and hit Wes with it'.

READER RESPONSES

I can't believe Duncan 'Disorderly' Ferguson didn't make it into your Worst (surely 'Best'?) Examples of Footballers Behaving Badly. This is a man who nuts old people in the street (a taxi rank in Stirling actually), gets done for drink-driving the night before his first Mersey derby and who tried to set fire to a pile of laundry in the Scotland squad hotel in Sweden at Euro 92.
Phil Baron, Bradford

01 FRANNY LEE TAKES ON NORMAN HUNTER
Baseball Ground, 1 November 1975

A case of the pitbull savaging the rottweiler. Hunter's hard-man reputation didn't intimidate the smaller, but equally combative, Francis Lee when the two clashed during a First Division match at the Baseball Ground. After exchanging blows (Hunter split Lee's lip with a left-hook), the ex-England internationals were sent off by referee Derek Nippard. But, with Lee considering business very much unfinished, the pair re-engaged fisticuffs all the way to the dressing room, pausing only when they were joined by both sets of players looking to slug it out.

02 DENNIS RODMAN'S HEADBUTT
Chicago, 16 March 1996

The baddest boy in the NBA never did anything quietly. Having been ejected from the Chicago Bulls' clash with the New Jersey Nets, Rodman's reaction was more colourful than his bright yellow Afro. After gesturing with his hands down the front of his shorts, Rodman concluded his argument with referee Ted Bernhardt by headbutting him above the left eye. Not content with his deftly delivered Glasgow kiss, Rodman proceeded to rip his own shirt off and march around the court, kicking over a water-cooler for good measure. It landed him a $20,000 fine – probably about the same as his annual hair-dye bill – and a six-game suspension.

03 DENNIS LILLEE'S ALUMINIUM BAT
Perth, 14 December 1979

If the big Australian was looking for a reaction as he walked to the crease in the first Ashes Test with an aluminium bat tucked under his arm, he got one. A stand-up row with England captain Mike Brearley ensued, with a bullish Lillee arguing that the rulebook didn't state a bat must be made of willow. Brearley, not surprisingly, opined that this just wasn't cricket. Some 10 minutes and an intervention from Australia captain Greg Chappell later, a furious Lillee relented and flung the offending lump of metal fully 40 yards towards the pavilion. He made 18 with its conventional replacement.

04 ERIC CANTONA'S KUNG-FU KICK
Selhurst Park, 25 January 1995

The most famous kick that Cantona ever delivered wasn't a sublime chip or a match-winning penalty, but a two-footed karate kick. The volatile Frenchman had just been sent off, four minutes into the second half of Manchester United's Premiership match against Crystal Palace, for kicking out at defender Richard Shaw. As Cantona headed for his early bath, 20-year-old Palace fan Matthew Simmons rushed down the stands to taunt the United player. Cantona leaped into action and then followed up his stunning horizontal assault with a more orthodox flurry of punches. The incident saw him banned from football for eight months. Oh, and the game ended 1–1.

05 THE BATTLE OF SANTIAGO
Santiago de Chile, 2 June 1962

David Coleman introduced the highlights of Chile's 2–0 World Cup win over Italy thus: 'Good evening. The game you are about to see is the most stupid, appalling, disgusting and disgraceful exhibition of football, possibly in the history of the game.' The man whose sending-off sparked the infamous 'Battle of Santiago' was Italy's Giorgio Ferrini. The game's first foul came within 12 seconds and, following an agricultural challenge, Ferrini was ordered off inside eight minutes. The match was delayed for several minutes before English referee Ken Aston, helped by several armed policemen, managed to bustle Ferrini off the pitch. 'I wasn't reffing a football match,' Aston said later. 'I was acting as an umpire in military manoeuvres.'

06 RIJKAARD SPITS IN VOLLER'S MULLET
Milan, 24 June 1990

Having narrowly missed the German striker's silver mullet once already, Frank Rijkaard's second attempt was right on target. The spat that led to the spit had been building from the moment that Rijkaard upended Rudi Voller after 20 minutes of Holland's World Cup second-round match against Germany. Moments later, Voller, who was highly agitated by this point, tried to wrestle the ball from the grasp of Dutch keeper Hans van Breukelen at a free kick. Rijkaard took exception and, after a melee, the pair were sent off. It was then that the Dutchman's second phlegm missile found its target and hung from Voller's hair like a bauble. The incident brought a new meaning to the phrase 'early bath'.

07 KEEGAN AND BREMNER'S BUST-UP
Wembley, 10 August 1974

Seething that he'd been butted in the Charity Shield (of all things) but unaware that Johnny Giles was the guilty party, Keegan focused his aggression on the most likely culprit – Leeds captain Billy Bremner. Not one to duck a fight, Bremner began trading blows with Keegan as if they were having a playground punch-up, which ensured that they became the first players to be sent off at Wembley. It didn't end there. Aggrieved that they'd been dismissed for fighting (it was the seventies, remember), they removed their shirts and threw them to the ground in disgust, walking off bare-chested. Each was fined £500 and banned for 11 games. Eight of which were for the shirt-throwing.

08 MARTY MCSORLEY ICES OPPONENT
Vancouver, 21 February 2000

Ice hockey doesn't do handbags at ten paces, as Donald Brashear found out when he upset Marty McSorley. The Boston Bruins' enforcer exacted revenge on Brashear with just 2.7 seconds of the NHL game remaining. McSorley swung his stick, two-handed, and smashed Brashear in the temple with such force that the Vancouver Canucks forward was left unconscious and twitching on the ice. McSorley's instant ejection was accompanied by jeers, plastic bottles and a police charge. Although found guilty of assault with a weapon, McSorley wasn't sentenced to jail. 'I got too carried away,' he said later. 'It was a dumb play.'

09 JUAN MARICHAL COMES OUT SWINGING
Candlestick Park, 25 August 1965

'I expected Marichal to attack me in some way – I had studied karate, and I was ready to annihilate him,' Dodger catcher John Roseboro said of the moment he threw the ball a little too close to Marichal's head. Marichal turned around to confront Roseboro, who stood up and took off his mask. Sensing he was about to get thumped himself, Marichal immediately hit the catcher over the head with his bat, opening a two-inch gash in Roseboro's scalp. With blood gushing down Roseboro's face, the two teams brawled for 14 minutes. Marichal was suspended for nine games, and Roseboro later sued him for $110,000 in damages. Apparently the two men became friends in the eighties.

10 MR & MRS TARANGO
Wimbledon, 1 July 1995

A self-dismissal. Upset by an umpire he considered 'the most corrupt official in the game', American tennis journeyman Jeff Tarango (whose previous Wimbledon best didn't exist – he'd lost 18 straight sets and six first-round ties) took issue with Bruno Rebeuh over a line-call during his third-round match against Alexander Mronz and walked out. Shaking with rage while packing away his rackets, Tarango rounded on the crowd (who were slow-handclapping him), telling them to 'shut up', before marching off. His wife Benedicte added the finishing touch by slapping Rebeuh as he made his way back to the changing room.

01 JORGE CAMPOS'S GOALKEEPING SHIRTS

'I've been looking for new kitchen curtains for a long time,' said former Norway keeper Erik Thorstvedt after swapping jerseys with Campos during the 1994 World Cup. One has to question Erik's taste in kitchen furnishings but you take his point. The flamboyant Mexican, his country's top keeper until recently, has an irrefutable claim on our No. 1 spot: he designs his own outfits ('Growing up surfing in Acapulco influenced me') making him the most dangerous fashion criminal on this list, and a serial offender with it.

02 MAUREEN DRAKE'S LEOPARDSKIN DRESS

Canada's fifth-best women's tennis players (ranked 123rd in the world) sported a leopardskin-and-gold fiasco at the Ericsson Open in March 2001, for her match against Martina Hingis. 'My coach said I had to wear it, and I'm making up all these excuses not to,' Drake said. 'But I had told her before that I'd wear it when I was playing a top 10 player because it was like I was on the hunt. So I wore it and the whole crowd just started whistling when I came out. I first wore it in Egypt and people were coming up to me telling me that I looked like Cleopatra.' (The outfit failed to work any magic – Hingis beat Drake 6–1, 6–4.)

03 KIRK STEVENS'S WHITE SUIT

In at three – and the spitting image of Dirk Diggler, porn-star hero of Boogie Nights – is snooker's 'Man in the White Suit', a player who once admitted being 'hopelessly addicted' to cocaine. How does Stevens defend his sartorial judgement? 'I only wore the white suit as my black one was dirty, but after that I couldn't wear anything else as people expected it.'

04 ANDRE AGASSI'S 'HOT LAVA' LOOK

A late-80s classic: think 'young Peter Stringfellow found living in Florida trailer park'. The Las Vegan has sobered considerably since then but, at the start of his career, a serious Day-Glo habit threatened to overshadow his prodigious tennis ability. 'All image and no substance' is how Agassi described his old self in an interview with *OSM*.

05 PORSCHE'S 'PINK PIG'

Porsche's 'Pink Pig' – it ran at Le Mans in 1971 but failed to finish – is a prime example of German humour gone wrong, and motor sport's ultimate fashion faux pas. The stylists at Porsche decided that because the design was so wide and squat the car should resemble a pig. They divided the body into sections and labelled each as if they were butcher's cuts. Martini Racing, under whose banner the car was running, did not take kindly to the porky motif though and elected not to place any of their logos on the car.

06 THE 1999 USA RYDER CUP TEAM

Choosing an example of a golfing fashion disaster is to construct a sentence involving the words 'fish' and 'barrel', but this horrific burgundy, cream and sepia creation represents the nadir. At the request of their captain Ben Crenshaw, the US team's shirts for the final day's play at Brookline in 1999 were decorated with pictures of past Ryder Cup-winning teams, designed to inspire the flag-waving patriots in the team (ie, most of them) to go out and whup some European tail. Asked about his opponents' choice of shirt, European captain Mark James deadpanned, 'I guess we missed out on that.'

07 WEST INDIES WORLD SERIES UNIFORM

In the late seventies Kerry Packer's World Series Cricket, the first foray into the pyjama game, inflicted this pink shocker on the unfortunate players of the West Indies. 'It's hardly the colour for the macho men from the Caribbean' was Viv Richards' unimpressed response to the uniform. Respected West Indian writer and broadcaster Tony Cozier went even further, saying, 'It is a colour which carries strong homosexual overtones in the Caribbean.' These days the West Indies play their one-day cricket in masculine maroon.

08 JORGE PAEZ'S SHORTS

The second loco Mexican on this list, a former feather-weight world champion, was born into a circus family, which explains his penchant for clownish outfits. This one, sported by Paez for his 1992 bout against journeyman

Brian Brown, is best described as *Swan Lake* meets *Last of the Mohicans*, and is typical of the Mexican's quixotic style; other outfits Paez has worn in the ring include a bridal gown, a Los Angeles Kings ice-hockey uniform, and top hat, tails and cane.

09 LINFORD CHRISTIE'S LYCRA SUITS

Another serial offender and a champion of the all-in-one lycra suit, the more attention-grabbing the better. That said, Linford won his fair share of races, so maybe he was on to something…

10 ICE SKATERS… ALL OF THEM

The ISU, ice skating's governing body, have a regulation which states that competitors' clothing must be 'Modest, dignified and appropriate for athletic competition, not garish or theatrical in design.' It's impossible to single out one skater to place on this list – they all tend to blatantly flout the rule book and dress up like actors in an amateur dramatics performance of Chekov. And this an Olympic sport.

READER RESPONSES

As an Aussie abroad, and living in London, I saw *OSM's* Fashion Disasters and was, quite frankly, amazed at the lack of a mention for our great sport of Aussie Rules Football. Those guys wear shorts which contravene the Trade Descriptions Act – they're more like hot pants. And as for their sleeveless shirts, which come in a range of vomit-inducing colour combinations, the less said the better. If the Village People were Australian, one of them would be an Aussie Rules player. An astonishing omission, guys. You should be ashamed of yourselves.
**Bradley Stringer,
Notting Hill, London**

As an American I have to chime in and place my vote for the USA's disgusting denim kit at the '94 World Cup. I still have nightmares of Alexi Lalas's flaming orange beard clashing with this atrocity.
**Michael Cartwright,
via email**

01 MUHAMMAD ALI V JOE FRAZIER

It began in 1971 in the build-up to the first of their three momentous collisions, when Ali called Frazier stupid, inarticulate, 'too ugly to be the champ' and 'an Uncle Tom'. For Ali, who always abused his opponents, it may have been standard fare. For Frazier it opened a 30-year-old wound. He denounced Ali as a draft-dodger and continued to call him Cassius Clay, his pre-conversion name. After both retired, many attempts were made to effect a reconciliation, but time did nothing to assuage Frazier's sense of grievance – even after Ali developed Parkinson's disease. 'They want me to love him,' Frazier said in 1996, 'but I'll open up the graveyard and bury his ass when the good Lord chooses to take him.' In March 2001, however, Ali finally apologised, and there were signs that the feud may be ending. 'I said a lot of things in the heat of the moment that I shouldn't have said,' Ali admitted. 'Called him names I shouldn't have called him. I'm sorry. It was all meant to promote the fight.' Frazier is said to have accepted the apology.

02 DON BRADMAN V BILL O'REILLY

Bradman may have been the greatest cricketer of them all, but he also knew how to bear a grudge – against enemies real and imagined. None more so than against Bill O'Reilly. O'Reilly was of Catholic Irish extraction, and the leader of a group of easygoing, sociable players in the Australian side. He epitomised everything Bradman – a Protestant who rarely drank – wasn't. As a result the great Australia side of the 1930s and 1940s was racked by internal feuding. Bradman vindictively and prematurely ended the career of arguably the greatest bowler of all time in a purge of his dressing-room enemies. O'Reilly and fellow clique member Jack Fingleton, who both loathed Bradman, exacted some public retribution later through their journalism.

03 TONYA HARDING V NANCY KERRIGAN

Despite being from different sides of the track – Harding was the rough girl with an alcoholic mother and layabout father, Kerrigan the well-spoken 'nice girl' with a blind mother – America's two foremost ice skaters were just friendly rivals. To start with. Then, in 1994, a mystery man in black whacked Kerrigan on the knee with a piece of lead piping weeks before the Winter Olympics. Jeff Gilooly, Harding's on-off husband, plotted the attack. He and his three co-conspirators said Harding knew about, and approved of, the assault. She denied it. The ensuing 'Skate-gate' scandal mesmerised the world. 'Afterwards, Nancy stayed at the tournament and I remember I gave her a hug,' Harding said in her interview with *OSM* in December 2000, 'and said I was sorry for what happened to her. Not because

I'd done anything wrong, of course. I was just sorry for her.' Ironically, it didn't do Kerrigan's career much harm. 'It's fair to say she's become the most recognisable skater in the world,' Kerrigan's husband and agent Jerry Solomon says. However, she and Harding have never made up and a televised reconciliation in 1997 failed. They haven't spoken since. Harding still receives hate mail.

04 GABRIELA SZABO V VIOLETA BECLEA-SZEKELY

These outstanding Romanian distance runners really hate each other. It began as a track rivalry when the younger, prettier Szabo (*right*) emerged in the 1990s to challenge Beclea's dominance. Cutting remarks by Szabo when Beclea failed a 1996 drugs test didn't help. Then when Szabo won the 1,500m at the 1999 world indoor championships, she pointedly ignored the offer of a congratulatory hand from Beclea, who had come second. Szabo's claim in a *Playboy* interview that the organisers of a meeting thought Beclea too 'ugly' to invite marked a lowpoint in their mutual antagonism. Beclea refused to accept Szabo's half-hearted apology and is suing for £100,000 damages. She may yet have the last laugh – in Romania, libel is punishable by up to two years in jail.

05 IAN BOTHAM V IAN CHAPPELL

It began in the bar of the Melbourne Hilton in 1977. Botham overheard Chappell slagging off England. He warned the 'Aussie loudmouth' three times to stop, then threw a punch, sending him sprawling off his bar stool and over a table of Aussie Rules footballers. When Chappell made one last jibe as he left, bulldog Botham chased him into the street; only the arrival of a police car prevented further violence. Over the years they continued to trade verbal punches. 'He was a good cricketer, nothing special,' Chappell said of Botham. 'As a human being he is a nonentity,' Botham responded. Chappell reopened hostilities in 1996 by claiming England's greatest all-rounder had threatened to cut him 'from ear to ear' with a beer glass; Botham denied it.

06 SEBASTIAN COE V LINFORD CHRISTIE

Britain's two most successful track athletes of recent times were uneasy bedfellows when they were team-mates in the 1980s. Coe, a double Olympic gold medallist, thought Christie was argumentative and disruptive, while the sprinter saw Coe as aloof and superior. For years those within the sport have known of their strained relationship. But that long-simmering mutual dislike erupted publicly when Coe accused the 1992 Olympic 100m gold medallist of being a difficult, 'boorish' whinger who was 'lucky' to have avoided a drugs ban at the Seoul Games in 1988 and was only made British team captain to keep him quiet. In response, Christie claimed Coe was now profiteering from the sport which made his name and fortune, and branded him a racist.

07 BENNY 'KID' PARET V EMILE GRIFFITH

Probably the most chilling feud of all. Animosity grew between these two rivals for boxing's world welterweight crown 40 years ago. Paret, a tough Cuban, lost his title to Griffith, a mild-mannered ex-milliner from the Virgin Islands, then regained it in a fight that was suspected of being a fix. At the weigh-in for their third showdown, in 1962, Paret called his opponent a homosexual and threatened to beat up both him and his 'husband'. Griffith was, understandably, furious. In the 12th round of their bout he trapped Paret on the ropes and battered him relentlessly. However, the referee didn't intervene – the Cuban was known to feign injury – and Paret lost consciousness, then died a few days later. A feud he had initiated had, tragically, cost him his life in what was one of boxing's first televised fatalities.

08 RICHARD COCKERILL V NORM HEWITT

Cockerill, the England hooker, fell out with his New Zealand opposite number when they went eyeball-to-eyeball during the haka at Old Trafford in 1997. After the first Test in Dunedin in June 1998, the pair took their loathing a stage further during a late-night, drink-fuelled scrap. Blows were traded both inside and outside a taxi, and Cocky (by nickname and by nature) was left nursing a black eye. The tussle highlighted a general feud between the England and All Black teams on that tour, which involved violent play and insult-trading by rival coaches Clive Woodward and John Hart.

09 NATALIE TAUZIAT V AMELIE MAURESMO

Mauresmo made her name with sensational play at the 1999 Australian Open when, as a 19-year-old, she beat Lindsay Davenport en route to the final. But the French teenager's muscular frame also attracted attention, with

Martina Hingis labelling her 'half a man'. Tauziat went further, attacking her lesbian compatriot's sexuality, and then, in her book *The Underside of Women's Tennis*, deriding Mauresmo for staging too many public displays of affection with her partner, Sylvie Bourdon. Mauresmo got her revenge by refusing to play in the Sydney Olympics if Tauziat was selected. Tauziat was dropped and Mauresmo played.

10 SIR ALEX FERGUSON V ALAN GREEN

When Ferguson became manager of Manchester United in 1986, these two actually became friends – Green would invite him to the BBC to watch live feeds of Scottish teams in action. It didn't last though. According to Green, one of Radio Five Live's leading commentators, Fergie's success at United made him much less tolerant of his opinionated ways. Green claimed in his recent book that Ferguson had become a 'foul-mouthed, arrogant, aggressive control freak' and a 'shocking bully'. Fergie hasn't spoken to Green since 1993 and has not gone public on the feud – although he did once remind the abrasive Irishman: 'You don't pick my fucking teams.'

READER RESPONSES

Your 10 sporting feuds possessed one glaring absentee. Croatian midfielder Robert Prosinecki and coach Miroslav Blazevic have had a 15-year feud which began when Blazevic saw Prosinecki play football as a young boy and declared: 'If this boy becomes a professional footballer, I'll eat my coaching certificate.' Prosinecki proved Blazevic wrong. Blazevic got his own back though, when he was national team coach of Croatia for the 1998 World Cup. Prosinecki helped his team get to the semi-final but the day before the match against host nation France, Prosinecki was dropped. He described it as 'the most humiliating moment of my career'. He retired from international football after France '98 (although he did make a comeback last year when Blazevic was still the coach).

Neil Billingham, London

THE TEN BIGGEST SPORTING CRYBABIES

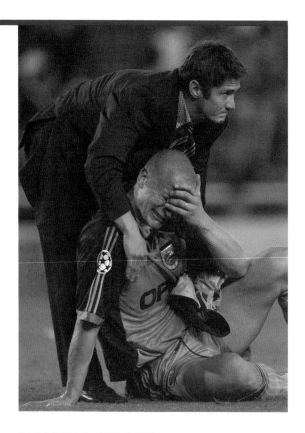

01 CARSTEN JANCKER

He cried, we laughed. How ironic that a German footballer should provide us with sport's finest example of Schadenfreude. The huge, shaven-headed Jancker is perhaps the last man on the planet you'd expect to blub like a five-year-old girl who's lost her favourite dolly – but then if you'd had the Champions League trophy snatched from your hands in the dying seconds, as Bayern Munich did against Man Utd in 1999, maybe you'd cry too.

02 JANA NOVOTNA

If an emotional sports star is looking for a well-padded shoulder to cry on, they need look no further than the Duchess of Kent – the caring, sharing royal who doesn't mind the odd tear leaking on to her twinset. And boy did Jana Novotna need a shoulder after an almighty choke which saw her throw away a 4–1 lead in the final set of the 1993 Wimbledon final against Steffi Graf. As Novotna waited for the presentation ceremony, her distress was obvious. The duchess gamely comforted her but Novotna couldn't stop the tears flowing as the weight of the occasion on Centre Court overwhelmed her.

03 OLIVER MCCALL

It might be unwise to call a former boxing world champion (and a heavyweight at that) a crybaby – and even unfair given McCall's fragile mental state at the time of this fight, in 1997 – but what the hell . . . The American fighter, who had KO'd Lennox Lewis with a right-hand from nowhere in their first bout in 1994, behaved in the strangest manner ever seen inside a boxing ring. Referee Mills Lane called time in the fifth round after the unfortunate McCall, seemingly unable – or unwilling – to throw any punches of his own, broke down in tears. 'For a few seconds I did half-believe he was trying to con me,' said Lewis after the fight. 'But then I saw his eyes and they weren't the eyes of a fighter…and the tears were pouring down his cheeks.'

04 MIKA HAKKINEN

Finns are generally considered a fearless, ice-cool bunch – they're not the sort of people likely to pull out a hanky during the potter's-wheel scene in *Ghost*. So when Mika Hakkinen crashed out of the Italian Grand Prix in 1999 – and thought, wrongly as it turned out, that his retirement signalled the end of his world title chances – he nipped into the bushes for a good old cry, obviously not wanting to show up his tough Finnish ancestors by blubbing in public. Unfortunately for Hakkinen, his cover was blown when a helicopter overhead filmed the whole episode.

05 TONYA HARDING

Unlike, for example, Oliver McCall, it's hard to sympathise with Harding – so we won't. This was, after all, the woman widely reviled after her arch rival, Nancy Kerrigan, was nobbled. So when the lace on Harding's right boot snapped at the start of her free-skating programme in the 1994 Winter Olympics, goodwill was bound to be in short supply. The judges in Lillehammer permitted Harding to fix her boot and skate again (she finished down in eighth place and never looked like challenging for the medals), although sceptics thought she had faked the tears in a bid to get the judges – and of course the public – back on her side. Whether the tears were real or not, they didn't work.

06 GARRY HERBERT

The coxed-pairs final in the 1992 Barcelona Olympics was well under way when Herbert, a small cox with a big voice, had an urgent word with his crew, Greg and Johnny Searle.

'Do you want to make a little bit of magic?' he shouted. The Searles obviously did and stormed to victory with a dramatic late surge. As the British national anthem played, Herbert couldn't hold back the tears. He stood in front of the giant brothers crying his eyes out, in the manner of a first-former who has just had his dinner money taken by the school bullies.

07 PAUL GASCOIGNE

'I looked at the fans and they were singing my name and it made me cry,' Gazza told *OSM* in 2002, when asked about the moment which made him famous around the world. The England midfielder didn't stop there though – after the painful World Cup semi-final defeat to Germany, he turned on the waterworks again. 'In the dressing room I was crying like mad,' he admitted. Thirteen years later, however, Gazza seems to have come to terms with the moment that defined his career: 'The people who joke about it, I always say to them, "When I was crying at the World Cup in 1990, where were you?"'

08 MARY DECKER

Decker, the glamour girl of American athletics in the eighties, was considered a near-certainty to win the 3,000m at the 1984 LA Olympics – and no one could argue that she didn't deserve a slice of luck after missing both the 1976 Games in Montreal (through injury) and the 1980 Games in Moscow (because of the US boycott). And had it not been for the pesky heel of barefooted Zola Budd, Decker would probably have been crying tears of joy on the winners' podium. (So either way she would have a decent claim to making this list.) As it was, though, the tears which came as Decker lay injured on the trackside were born out of the knowledge that she had been cruelly denied Olympic glory once again.

09 NICK FALDO

It was easy to admire Nick Faldo and his relentless quest for the perfect swing, but he was often a difficult man to love – he worked on his golf much more than he worked on his charm. One of the rare occasions when Faldo let down his emotional guard, though, was at the 1992 Open, at Muirfield. Trailing American John Cook by two shots on the final day, and with just four holes to play, Faldo somehow found the inner strength to play the best golf of his life and steal a dramatic victory. On shaky legs, he sank the final putt and could hold himself together no longer. For a strapping six-footer, Faldo's tears – like Carsten Jancker's – seemed rather girlish, but they did his public image no harm at all.

10 DEREK REDMOND

Sport's equivalent of watching Bambi's mother die. Not many moments on this list – if any – remain so poignant that they can reduce grown men to tears, but this is a bona fide weepie. The spectacle of Redmond's father, Jim, rushing down from the stands – slaloming around jobsworth officials as he went – to help his hamstrung son finish his 400m semi-final at the 1992 Olympics in Barcelona is one of the most touching episodes in sport. As Redmond later recalled: 'It made quite an impact because everyone seemed to think I demonstrated the perfect Olympic spirit…not the winning but the taking part.' I'm welling up, so I'm going to stop writing now.

READER RESPONSES

Why no Alex Higgins? Higgins is often berated, yet his first world title saw an overwhelming flow of joyful tears - unseen before by the likes of Ray Reardon and Doug Mountjoy, and never repeated by Steve Davis or Stephen Hendry. An unashamed display of emotional fragility, hidden deep within this fascinating man.
**D.C. Kneath,
Swansea**

01 GIANT HAYSTACKS 686lb

It is said that in every fat man there is a thin man battling to get out. In the case of Giant Haystacks, however, there was an entire rugby team. Hailing from a family of Irish giants – his grandfather was 7ft 5in – Haystacks tipped the scales at 49 stones and made his arch-rival, the so-called 'Big' Daddy (an elfin 28 stones in comparison) look like Calista Flockhart on the Atkins Diet. After the golden days of British grappling ended, Haystacks (Martin Ruane to his friends) took his unique brand of thuggery to the States, where he attempted to carve a new wrestling career as the 'Loch Ness Monster'. Prior to his death from cancer in 1998, he ran a debt collection agency in Manchester – defaulters were threatened with splash-downs and half-Nelsons.

02 KONISHIKI 660lb

Nicknamed 'The Dump Truck', Hawaiian-born Konishiki weighed in at a quarter of a ton. To put that in some kind of perspective, fighting him was like trying to shove five Darren Andertons out of the ring. The original immovable object, he enjoyed a 15-year career in sumo and became the first foreign wrestler to win three Grand Sumo titles and achieve the coveted *ozeki* ranking. And, thanks to *chankonabe* – the special high-calorie sumo diet of eating just about everything in sight – he also became the first wrestler to break through the 600lb mark. Such feats brought the Dump Truck fame, fortune and celebrity status, and also helped him net a seven-stone model wife. Remarkably, she is still alive.

03 ERIC 'BUTTERBEAN' ESCH 425lb

A former assembly-line worker, IBA Super-Heavyweight champion Eric 'Butterbean' Esch's success in boxing is based on a peculiar motivational technique – he imagines that the man in the opposite corner is trying to steal the food from his mouth. 'I have the urge to win just like I have the urge to eat ice cream,' he maintains. Unlike many of his less prudent contemporaries, the King of the Four Rounders has taken his prize money and invested it in his very own steak house – Mr Beans in Curry, Alabama. Highlight of the extensive menu, apparently, is 'The Butterbean', a speciality steak weighing in at an artery-clogging 2lb.

04 WILLIAM PERRY 370lb

When William 'The Refrigerator' Perry barged his way into the world of gridiron in the mid-1980s, his arrival was heralded as the 'the best use of fat since the invention of bacon'. As the hulk at the heart of the Chicago Bears defense, Perry used every last bit of his 370lb frame and 22in neck to destructive effect, helping the Bears to their record-breaking Super Bowl success in January 1986. Now 40 and nudging 400lb, the Fridge is still competing at the highest level; he recently took part in the World Hot Dog Eating Championship.

05 WILLIAM FOULKE 350lb

At 6ft 6in, William Foulke is the tallest footballer ever to have represented England. At some way over 20 stones, he is also the heaviest. Imaginatively nicknamed 'Fatty' by friends and fans alike, Foulke made his international debut in the 4–0 drubbing of Wales on 29 March 1897, and in the days when keepers didn't have to stay on their line for spot-kicks, his penalty-saving technique was a sight to behold. As the taker approached the ball, Foulke would charge off his line. The mere sight of the gargantuan frame bearing down on them was usually enough not just to block out any sight of the goal but to render the taker paralysed by fear. As Foulke's fame spread, so did his waistline. In 1892, he weighed in at a cuddly 15 stones; by 1901 he had ballooned to 21 stones. When he eventually retired in 1907 he tipped the scales (or rather flattened them) at a colossal 25 stones. And you thought Neville Southall was on the tubby side. After his retirement he was asked if he objected to people calling him 'Fatty'; to which he replied: 'You can call me what you like. Just don't call me late for dinner.'

06 TREVOR MISAPEKA 300lb

Described by the press, somewhat inaccurately, as 'burly' and a 'sprinter' – he was fat and a shot-putter – Trevor Misapeka arrived at the 2001 World Athletics Championships in Edmonton, Canada only to find that as he hadn't met the qualifying standard for the shot putt he couldn't compete. With time on his hands, the 21-stone American Samoan entered himself in the 100m sprint heats (that didn't require a qualifying time) and took his place in Heat One wearing an old capped-sleeve T-shirt and an ordinary pair of street trainers. Nearly 14.5 seconds later, Misapeka crawled over the finishing line in last place. That said, it was a personal best for the baker's son. 'It was a new event for me,' he said later. 'I've never run the 100m before.'

07 W.G. GRACE 280lb

Despite advocating the many benefits of temperance in diet and regular sleep and exercise, the good doctor's playing weight still rocketed from a lean 167lb to over 280lb during the course of his illustrious cricketing career. When he took to the crease, Grace looked like he was sporting the kind of all-over-body armour that modern-day players hide behind. In fact, the only padding he ever had or needed were the several layers of flesh rolling under his whites.

08 BABE RUTH 235lb

Despite possessing a pie-shaped face and the physique of an orang-utan, the Sultan of Swat's domination of baseball was total, and his reputation as a foul-mouthed, hard-drinking gutbucket did little to temper the American public's insatiable desire to see him perform. Ruth's off-field antics often attracted more coverage than his record-breaking endeavours on it: the 17-stone Babe liked to punch umpires and throw dirt in their faces, chase hecklers through the stands and dangle disrespectful team-mates from the windows of speeding trains. Those who knew Ruth have said the All-American hero had a marked tendency to belch at inappropriate moments, but then if you breakfasted on whisky, hot dogs and bicarbonate of soda, you'd belch too.

09 BILL WERBENIUK 290lb

It is the Embassy World Snooker Championships, April 1983. Willie Thorne is playing Bill Werbeniuk, the so-called 'Walrus from Winnipeg'. As the colossal Canadian bends down to take his shot, his long-suffering trousers finally give in to the enormous stress placed on them by his vast buttocks and split right up the back. Matters are compounded when Thorne realises his 20-stone opponent has decided to go commando for the day. 'It wasn't a pretty sight,' was all a visibly distressed Thorne would later say of the incident.

10 TONY GALENTO 242lb

At his peak in the 1930s, Tony 'Two Ton' Galento routinely prepared for his fights by pulling up a stool at the bar in New York's Plaza Hotel and feasting on hamburgers, hot dogs and cigars. Yet he was one hell of a boxer. In his fight against Joe Louis at the Yankee Stadium in June 1939, Galento made the fundamental mistake of putting his opponent on his backside, only for Louis to pick himself up off the canvass and turn Galento's face into what one press wag called 'the world's biggest plate of spaghetti'. As his career and weight went in opposite directions, Galento tried his hand at refereeing bear-wrestling bouts and boxing kangaroos and octopuses ('It took 50 minutes to get the gloves on the octopus,' he said). Though he never weighed two tons – that would be madness – Galento was nevertheless sufficiently concerned about his weight that he once embarked on a diet of bread, water and vitamins. 'In 14 days,' he concluded, 'I lost two weeks.'

THE TEN DODGIEST HAIRCUTS IN THE HISTORY OF FOOTBALL

01 RUDI VOLLER

Peter Shilton paid for his in champagne, Terry McDermott, Phil Thompson, Graeme Souness, Kevin Keegan and Craig Johnston greased theirs daily, but Rudi Voller was, and remains, queen of the perm. Peroxide with grey highlights, Voller's cut made him a German style icon and elevated him to the top of this competitive style category – landing him *OSM*'s overall worst cut prize. The style's greatest moment came when, during the 1990 World Cup, it collected and held, glue-like, the spit of Frank Rijkaard, leading to the Dutchman's famous red card. Voller remains one of the most popular men in Germany. He narrowly beats retired Austrian striker Toni Polster to the title – Polster wore his monster-perm with white socks and gold jewellery. He now has his own fashion label.

02 ALEXI LALAS

If you're going to be a ginger Detroit rocker-cum-foot-baller, you might as well look like this – which is why Lalas only makes second on the list. It's a shocking set of facial hair devices – but whatever you think about him, Lalas is totally true to himself: bad haircut, bad musician, bad foot-baller. He does, though, take some credit for spending two years in Italy with Padova (after aborting a move to Coven-try) without toning it down. He built a reputation in Serie A as a foul-mouthed New Age traveller, but enjoyed it. 'It was great, man, playing in Italy,' he explains. He gave up football in 1998 after meeting Pelé ('Fuck, I mean, he's the man, all that sort of stuff just blows me away') to work with his band full-time. His first major album, *Ginger*, was released in November that year. 'We just blew it out in two weeks in the studio,' he said. 'Man, it rocks.'

03 DAVID SEAMAN

Seaman has needed a haircut from a proper, sensible £8-a-go barber for the past 21 years. Instead, the England keeper uses the likes of Belgravia's Errol Douglas – a celebrity stylist – and turns up at grounds all over the country look-ing like a drug-weakened advertising executive in shorts. In 1998, he was named most stylish sports star at the *Elle* Style Awards. Five years on he's just a 40-year-old with a ponytail. On leather-loving Emmanuel Petit, Roberto Baggio and even snooker's Pete Ebdon, it didn't look so bad. On Seaman, it's a Soho porn merchant's dream.

04 JASON LEE

22 May 1996: the ultimate bad hair day. After a month of *Fantasy Football*'s Frank Skinner and David Baddiel link-ing Lee's pineapple hairdo to his poor performances (Lee was depicted in then-Forest manager Frank Clark's office failing to hit a tea cup with a sugar cube from six inches)

the striker was transfer-listed, and a promising career left in ruins. Richard & Judy invited him on to *This Morning* for a phone-in, Nottingham nightclubs put on themed pineapple nights, the press hounded his family and, by June, the BBC were receiving more than 200 letters a week with pictures of pineapples in different settings. Lee, who had been Forest's top scorer, suffered badly. 'It was unbelievable,' he said. 'It went on and on and my family were hammered.' He left on loan, before permanent moves to Watford then Chesterfield. Now, with a freshly shaved head, he's rebuilding his career at Peterborough.

05 GEORGE BERRY

The worst/best afro of all time – big, square and in your face. Today George Berry is a bald PFA executive, but in the seventies he was a bad haircut god, a Welsh international and considered by the rugby-playing Welsh wing of his Jamaican-Welsh family 'a big poof'. 'People think I had a square Afro, because it was so big it never fitted into photo frames and the papers and magazines had to crop it that way. There were plenty of big hairstyles around then – Remi Moses, Brendon Batson – but mine was the biggest and best.' Berry won a 1980 League Cup medal with Wolves, then moved on to Stoke, Aldershot and Stafford Rangers. Other exponents include the absurd Carlos Valderama – who ignored searing temperatures throughout his career to maintain his look – Alan Sunderland and the pre-bald Gianluca Vialli.

06 PETER BEARDSLEY

There's something heroic about Peter Beardsley's hair. Any boy sporting this cut to school would be broken in minutes – but Beardsley has stood by it for over 22 years. In 2000 he was tipped as a great lover by the *Sunday Mirror*, who claimed 'research shows that women find it hard to resist the charms of ugly men like Peter Beardsley. They try harder to make their partner happy.' Beardsley, though, was also once named 'only person who, when he appears on television, makes daleks hide behind the sofa'.

07 RALPH COATES

A haircut so good they made a song about it. 'Grease Your Ralph', released in 1987 by Welsh band the Abs (and still available from specialist shops) was a tribute to Coates's combover – the only football combover widely considered better than Bobby Charlton's. When Coates tore down Burnley's wing, his hair travelled a second or two behind him – Charlton rarely held his with the same panache. Nobby Stiles was similarly inclined – and Bobby Mikhailov, ex-Reading and Bulgaria, once named 'cutest goalkeeper' by Bulgarian fans, wore a wig during games. Now, of course, a good bald haircut, modelled on the old Beckham look, will set you back £300.

08 ALAN BILEY

Mullet king Alan Biley comes in eighth for being a leader of this defining trend: Paul Walsh, Ron and Paul Futcher, Gerry Francis, Barry Venison, Colin Hendry, Chris Waddle, king of camp Mark Lawrenson, Bulgarian werewolf Trifon Ivanov and the whole of Eastern Europe – for whom it became the cut of choice throughout the nineties – owe him a great debt. Today, Biley, a seventies peroxide mullet legend for Cambridge, Derby, Everton and Portsmouth, manages Dr Martens League side Spalding after spells as a nanny, a landscape gardener and a council worker. But a mullet isn't always a bad thing. In 1996, after Spain's top sex symbol Julen 'El Guapo' (gorgeous) Guerrero was forced to cut his mullet by Athletic Bilbao's owner, female fans besieged the San Mames stadium for two days in protest. Top mullet fact: the word mullet comes from the nineteenth-century term 'mullethead', meaning 'moron' or 'fool'. Today the style is worn by those who consider themselves ironic.

09 CLAUDIO CANIGGIA

Caniggia wins credit for maintaining this cut, not only for 15 years, but to the detriment of his career. Told by Argentina coach Daniel Passarella in 1995 to have his 'girl's hair' shortened or be thrown out of the squad, Caniggia – suspended for 13 months for cocaine use two years previously – chose the latter, and disappeared for six months. In 1998 his glam wife Marianna Nannis accused Diego Maradona of leading him astray: 'At times I believe Diego is in love with my husband,' she said. 'It must be the long hair and big muscles.' In October 2002, 7,000 blond-wig wearing Scots watched him score a home debut screamer for Dundee. The Caniggias moved to Glasgow shortly afterwards. Caniggia beats Derby's Taribo West, once master of Floella Benjamin bead chic, but now just a thinning Jason Lee wannabe.

10 SOCRATES

A fantastic player best known for chain-smoking at half-time, Brazilian legend Socrates was probably the hairiest man ever to feature in top-level football (apart from Richard Keys). A star of the 1982 and 1986 World Cup finals, Socrates, also a qualified doctor, was an outspoken political dissident with grooming to match. His sense of style earns him 10th spot – Everton troll Abel Xavier, Gazza's hair extensions and the wild man of hair Terry Hurlock all just miss out.

Published by Yellow Jersey Press in association
with Guardian Newspapers Ltd 2003

1 3 5 7 9 10 8 6 4 2

Copyright © Guardian Newspapers Ltd 2003

Guardian Newspapers Ltd has asserted its right under the Copyright,
Designs and Patents Act 1988 to be identified as the author of this work

The Guardian and The Observer are registered trademarks
of Guardian Newspapers Ltd

Page 4 constitutes an extension of these copyright notices

This book is sold subject to the condition that it shall not, by way of
trade or otherwise, be lent, resold, hired out, or otherwise circulated
without the publisher's prior consent in any form of binding or cover
other than that in which it is published and without a similar condition
including this condition being imposed on the subsequent purchaser

First published in book form in Great Britain in 2003 by
Yellow Jersey Press
Random House
20 Vauxhall Bridge Road
London SW1V 2SA

The Random House Group Limited Reg. No. 954009
www.randomhouse.co.uk

A CIP catalogue record for this book is available from the British Library

ISBN 0-224-07283-8

Printed and bound in Germany by
Äppl Druck, Wemding